796.425 CLER

BOSTON
MARATHON
HISTORY BY THE MILE

BOSTON
MARATHON
HISTORY BY THE MILE

PAUL C. CLERICI

THE
History
PRESS

Published by The History Press
Charleston, SC 29403
www.historypress.net

Boston Marathon®, BAA Marathon™, and the BAA unicorn logo are trademarks of the Boston Athletic Association. Use of these trademarks without written permission from the Boston Athletic Association is prohibited. *Boston Marathon History by the Mile* is not an official publication of the Boston Athletic Association.

Front cover, clockwise from top left: With bicyclists leading the way, and a few waiting on the sidewalk at right, the field of the third annual Boston Marathon in 1899 makes its way up the dirt road of Main Street in Ashland. *Courtesy Ashland Historical Society;* Located on the Center School grounds near Hopkinton Town Common is the *Yes You Can* statue of Team Hoyt, the inspirational multiple-sport duo of Dick Hoyt and his son Rick Hoyt, a spastic quadriplegic who lives with cerebral palsy. *Photo by Paul C. Clerici;* The streets of the Boston Marathon are filled in the early miles. *Jeff Johnson photo courtesy* New England Runner; The last mile marker—26 M—is located on Boylston Street, just 385 yards from the finish line. *Photo by Paul C. Clerici;* Nations' flags and thick crowds line the Boylston Street approach to the finish line. *Photo by Frank Clerici Sr.*

Back cover, from top: Throughout the Boston Marathon, spectators often keep runners updated on the score of the morning's Red Sox game. *Photo by Paul C. Clerici;* The *Spirit of the Marathon* statue, which peers over the course at one mile in Hopkinton, depicts 1946 Boston Marathon champion Stylianos Kyriakides on the left and the "spirit" of fellow Greek countryman Spyridon Louis, winner of the 1896 Olympic Marathon. *Photo by Paul C. Clerici;* At the Steven's Corner start line in 1912, the final start-line location in Ashland, Boston Marathon runners prepare for the sixteenth annual event. *Courtesy the Sports Museum of New England/Ashland Historical Society.*

First published 2014

ISBN 978-1-5402-1014-2

Library of Congress CIP data applied for.

I dedicate this book to my parents, Frank Clerici Sr. and Carol Hunt-Clerici; my brother and sister-in-law, Frank Clerici Jr. and Regina Clerici; and my late brother, David Clerici.

I wish to also dedicate this book to all the Boston Marathon athletes, volunteers, spectators, supporters, officials, media, and their families and friends for providing its strength, excitement, history, and enduring spirit.

CONTENTS

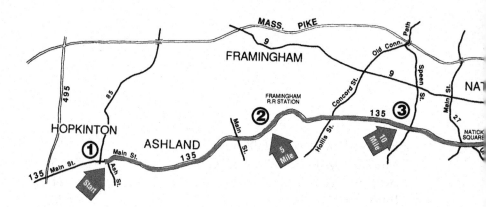

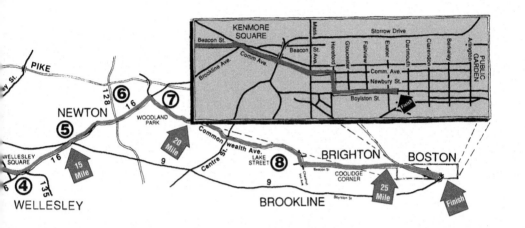

From west to east, the Boston Marathon course travels through eight towns and cities: Hopkinton, Ashland, Framingham, Natick, Wellesley, Newton, Brighton/Brookline, and Boston. *Courtesy* New England Runner.

FOREWORD

It is truly an honor and pleasure to have been asked by Paul Clerici to write a foreword for his new book, *Boston Marathon History by the Mile*. Having run and finished the Boston Marathon forty-one consecutive times (as of 2013), having helped to direct it for twenty-six years (as of 2013), having lived in a house right on the course, and having been up and down the course about a million times, I guess you could say I am quite intimate with every pothole and every streetlight that exists along the course!

People always ask me, "So, what makes Boston so special?"

Certainly the history and the tradition of the race come to mind right away. However, for me, it's also the course itself. There is just something very special about this course—it has character like no other one in the world that I have run (and I've run 128 marathons).

The quaint start in Hopkinton. The downhills through Ashland and into Framingham and across the railroad tracks. The Natick Town Common. And the cheering and hugging and kissing from the young ladies of Wellesley College cannot be described in words—you just have to experience it yourself.

The gradual "hill" no one plans for that goes right over Route 128 toward the Newton-Wellesley Hospital. Taking a right at the Newton Fire Station at seventeen and a half miles and taking on "the hills" of Newton, the last one being Heartbreak Hill. Passing the Johnny Kelley statue and then running past the roar of the Boston College students.

Then seeing the CITGO sign for the first time as you turn left onto Beacon Street with four miles to go. Crossing over the Mass Pike, seeing

Fenway Park to the right, crossing over the "One Mile to Go" mark painted on the road in Kenmore Square. And then the famous "right on Hereford, left on Boylston" and the final six hundred yards to the finish line at the Boston Public Library.

Oh, yes, and there are a few spectators along the 26.2-mile course to cheer you on!

I was seventeen when I ran my first "Boston." It wasn't pretty. And I was a bandi… a bandi…well, I just can't say that word. Let's just say that at the time, I was too young to officially enter; you had to be eighteen years old.

I collapsed in the Newton hills and was immediately transported to the Newton-Wellesley Hospital. My grandfather, who lived near the course, was waiting for me at Coolidge Corner. But I never arrived. He said he'd be back next year, waiting for me. Sadly, however, he died two months later.

I dedicated that race to him but once again dropped out at mile 21.5. Little did I know, though, that it was at that exact location where my grandfather was buried in the Evergreen Cemetery, right there on the marathon course. He said he would be there, and he was, spiritually. I finished the race that year and have every year since.

In 1987, there was a wheelchair division accident and an accident with the start of the race in which the lead runners tripped on the rope being held to hold the runners back before the gun fired. I was then offered the job as technical coordinator for the 1988 Boston Marathon. My conundrum was the decision to continue to run in the race or to help run—that is, direct—the race.

I took the job. That year, I simply imposed a controlled start for the wheelchair athletes and replaced the rope with a human chain of volunteers. Voila—problem fixed! And I have had the job for twenty-seven years.

At the conclusion of the 1988 marathon, my first year helping to manage the race, I decided to head back to the start and run the course myself, which I did and finished *last*, about eleven o'clock at night. I've been last in the race ever since; that is, for the past twenty-six years. But frankly, I am quite okay with that.

As for helping to direct the race, my fondest moment, other than that first year, was the 100th running of the race in 1996, when we had to figure out a way to get more than thirty-eight thousand runners across a startling line that is only thirty-nine feet wide. And we did—in less than thirty minutes.

Then there was a nor'easter in 2007, and we had to deal with a storm of "epic proportions," which we did. And then there was 2012, the "inferno" year, when temperatures reached almost ninety degrees. We almost cancelled the race the day before, but we asked the runners to take personal responsibility and offered them the choice to defer to the following year if they determined that it would just be too hot. We went ahead with the race and dealt with the heat as best we could.

Then came April 15, 2013.

We needed and deserved a good day, and it all started off magnificently. But then at 2:50 p.m., the day turned to violence and tragedy. Of course, no one could have predicted this. I was actually back in Hopkinton, getting ready to start my run, when I got the call. We rushed right back to Boston and got back in twenty minutes, going over one hundred miles per hour while being escorted by the Massachusetts State Police. What unfolded from there has been well documented. We then focused on a special 2014.

To run it and to run in it—what a privilege! No one else gets to do that.

When I first started to run it at night, I experienced a lot of hecklers—people saying things like, "Hey, you slug, train next year. Maybe you won't be last!" Two years ago, after having done this over twenty years in a row, one guy in a lounge chair with a beverage in his hand started yelling at me, telling me to pick it up and that the old man went by hours ago. His friend elbowed him and said, "Hey, leave him alone. That's the race director!" Ha, it took twenty-five years, but I'm somebody now—just like the other twenty-seven thousand runners who finished ahead of me!

God bless all the victims of the 2013 race. We will never forget you. And to Paul Clerici, congratulations on an outstanding job on this history-by-the-mile account of the Boston Marathon.

Dave McGillivray
BAA Boston Marathon Race Director
December 2013

FOREWORD

It's difficult for people today to understand how different it was and what I was up against in that first Boston Marathon in 1966. Before that run, it was generally believed that women were physically unable to run marathon distances. This is the key point. In those days, women were not expected to have careers, especially as doctors, lawyers, professors, or executives. Women were expected to marry, stay at home, and tend the children and the house—or perhaps work as telephone operators, secretaries, nurses, or elementary school teachers until they married.

Women who ran Boston before 1972 were in the yet-to-be-sanctioned women's open division. Women were/are not qualified to run in men's division races any more than men are qualified to run in women's division races—this is a fundamental rule of sporting events. At that time, per Amateur Athletic Union (AAU) rules, Boston had only a men's division race. After Title IX—the federal statute that prohibits discrimination on the basis of sex in public institutions, including the financing of sports and sports events—the AAU began to sanction long-distance races for women, and the Boston Athletic Association (BAA) set up the first officially sanctioned women's open division Boston Marathon in 1972.

In sports, women's track and field was nonexistent. Women were allowed to play tennis, golf, half-court basketball, lacrosse, field hockey, and volleyball in a lady-like fashion. And heaven forbid if a grown woman should run or perspire in public. Women were not allowed to compete at distances greater than one and a half miles, according to AAU rules. Running was almost unheard of even for men. There were no major-city marathons. Boston was about it. It's not as if there were dozens of well-trained women running marathon distances. Women didn't run. Women themselves didn't know they could run those distances because they were never allowed to. Even female coaches forbade their girls from running more than the prescribed distance, and women outside of sports would have no reason to do so.

In 1964, I first saw the Boston Marathon and fell in love with it. I loved to run and had discovered that running through the woods with the neighborhood dogs made me feel so relaxed, energized, and happy that I wished everyone could find this in their lives. At that time, I was running five miles simply because I loved to run; I wasn't thinking of running in races. When I saw Boston, I realized these runners felt the same way I did about running and about what it means to be human—the dignity and integrity it takes to run like this. Something inside me decided that I would run that race, just to be part of it. When I started, I wasn't thinking of making a statement. I wasn't thinking men or women. I wasn't even thinking of it as an athletic event. To me, it was a spring ritual, a celebration of life. I didn't know that women weren't allowed. I had no coach, no books, no encouragement. I just started to train myself the best I could, running in nurse's shoes, which were the only sturdy women's shoes I could find. I trained for two years.

In February 1966, I wrote to the BAA for my application, using my full name and not hiding my gender. I received a letter back from race director Will Cloney telling me that women were not physiologically able to run marathon distances, that the BAA couldn't take on the medical liability, and that, moreover, women were not allowed to run the Boston Marathon because it was a men's division event. At the time, I was running thirty miles at a stretch! It was at this point that I had to decide whether to give up my dream or to challenge the prevailing culture. I decided to challenge the culture. But I was in a double bind. How could I prove I could run the marathon if I wasn't allowed to run it? So I took the three-thousand-mile bus ride from my home in San Diego to Boston and arrived the day before the Marathon. My parents, who were living in Winchester, Massachusetts, thought I was delusional and that somehow I thought I was going to run Boston. My dad was very angry. He was afraid I'd hurt myself or even die if I tried to run it. I convinced my mother to drive me to the start in Hopkinton.

It is important to remember that the women's division marathon was not officially sanctioned yet, and with me being a woman, I was running in the first-ever yet-to-be-sanctioned women's division Boston Marathon. My purpose was to demonstrate that a woman could run a marathon and run it well. In 1966, I was the sole woman, and so by that very nature, the not-yet-sanctioned women's division race started wherever I started.

My mother let me out of the car about half a mile from the center of Hopkinton, and I began to run at that point. I ran to Hopkinton center, and I ran around the common, avoiding officials and policemen. I was going into the unknown. I knew I was doing something I was specifically forbidden from doing. I thought I might be arrested. But foremost in my mind was that I had to run. I couldn't be stopped. If I were prevented from running, I wouldn't be able to prove that a woman could run.

The men in those days started on the far side of the common. I ran around the starting pen, but I knew if I tried to get into the pen, I'd be detected and stopped. I found a hollow by a granite gatepost, surrounded by bushes on the other side of the common. Then I continued running for a half hour. As the time for the men's division race approached, I continued to run, and by this time I'd run somewhere between three and four miles. I stopped back in my hollow and waited for the men's division race to begin. I waited until about half the pack had gone by, and then I began to run again. It was at this point that I joined the men's division runners, and the as-yet-to-be-sanctioned women's division and the men's division continued on to Boston together.

I had the hood of my sweatshirt pulled up to conceal my femininity; however, the men quickly realized that I was a woman. They could have easily shouldered me out of the race, but they were friendly and supportive. Later, race official Jock Semple said he'd seen me running at the start but hadn't tried to stop me because I hadn't cheated to get an illegal number. I hadn't broken any rules. This myth that the men were against women running just isn't true. It was that no one knew that women could run that kind of distance. Not even women knew it.

I had a huge responsibility on my shoulders because I was making a statement and challenging the status quo. If I'd failed to finish, I would have confirmed all the prejudices against women and set women back another fifty years. I was there alone, making my statement. I drank no water or electrolytes for the entire race. My new boys' running shoes gave me blisters. Although I was on a sub-three-hour pace for most of the race, in the last two or three miles, my pace dropped off because of dehydration and the pain of the blisters.

Thousands of people saw me run and cheered me along the way. Reporters were following my run. A local radio station was broadcasting my progress. So people knew I was coming. When I got to Wellesley, the women were ecstatic. One of them cried, "Ave Maria! Ave Maria!" It was a huge thing. I ran all the way to Boston and finished in about 3:20:00, later calculated to be 3:21:40—ahead of two-thirds of the men! Massachusetts governor John Volpe came down to shake my hand. Reporters gathered around. It was a fantastically positive, amazing, pivotal event that changed social consciousness.

After the race, I took a taxi home to Winchester to find my house jammed with reporters and my parents looking totally bewildered as phone calls poured in congratulating them on their daughter. As I had hoped, my upbeat, non-threatening approach inspired men and women. Already, a representative from the AAU was talking about changing the rules so that women could run. It was exactly what I wanted to happen.

The following year, everyone knew a woman was going to run Boston. Reporters had been calling my parents for days. I had a flu and wasn't sure if I'd be able to run. But I realized that I had to run, sick or not, to dispel any remaining doubts in the minds of those who still couldn't believe a woman could run a marathon, let alone finish ahead of two-thirds of the men. In 1967, it was cold and drizzly, and there were two women in the not-yet-sanctioned women's division race: myself and Kathrine Switzer. I did not know at the time that she was in the race. I stood openly at the men's start, so this is where the second yet-to-be-sanctioned women's division race started. I waited until half the pack had left and then started running. Some distance into the race, I couldn't breathe, so I lay on someone's cold, wet lawn while they called a doctor. Suddenly, the cramp released, and to everyone's amazement, I sprang up and finished the race.

Regarding the photographs of an outraged Semple trying to grab the number on Switzer? In the technical sense, regardless of intent or circumstances, Switzer had obtained an illegal number in the men's division race, even though she was running in the as-yet-to-be-sanctioned women's division race based on the simple fact that she's a woman. As she was not an official runner, she did not have the required pre-race morning physical, and her run was not approved/sanctioned by the officials. Not everyone knows that the reason Semple was trying to remove the number was because he felt she had cheated the system to get it. To Semple, the presence of an unqualified runner in a sanctioned race jeopardized the accreditation of the race itself and threatened to invalidate the running times of the qualified participants. At the time, the incident so antagonized officials that all hope of opening the race to women vanished. Cloney commented that if women wanted to run a marathon, they should organize one of their own. The trouble was that the AAU rules precluded women's marathons. This had to change.

I finished first in 1967, to one side of the men's division finish, in a time of 3:27:17. In 1968, I finished first among five women. Sara Mae Berman won the yet-to-be-sanctioned women's division in 1969, 1970, and 1971. Our names are engraved on the Boston Marathon Centennial Monument in Copley Square, and the BAA has since awarded us medals for these wins. In 1972, Nina Kuscsik, who was instrumental in petitioning the AAU to allow women to run marathons, won Boston in 3:10:26.

Roberta "Bobbi" Gibb
First woman to run the Boston Marathon
December 2013

ACKNOWLEDGEMENTS

This book took over two decades to write. Well, maybe not literally, but physically. Along with the knowledge and experience accumulated from the millions of foot strikes and hundreds of miles on the Boston Marathon course from which I drew, there are many people whose own footprints helped make this book possible.

I want to truly thank Charles Bahne, Rich Benyo, Melissa Berczuk, Tom Burke, Will Collicott, Judy Conroy, Tom Derderian, Tabitha Dulla, Bob Fitzgerald, Jack Fleming, Steve Flynn, Bob Gee, Roberta "Bobbi" Gibb, Tim Kilduff, Maurice Kornreich, Leo Kulinski Jr., Michelle LeBrun, Patrick Leehey, Robert Levitsky, Ellie Malloy, Nick Martin, Jack McDonald, Dave McGillivray, Katie Parry, Toni Reavis, Donni Richman, Denise Robson, Jan Seeley, Coach Bill Squires, Edith Steblecki, Kathrine Switzer, Fred Treseler, and Andy Yelenak.

For research and reference, my grateful appreciation to the Archdiocese of Boston, *Arnoldia* (Harvard University), the Ashland Estate of Henry Clay, Ashland Historical Society, Ashland Sporting Association, Associated Press, Bank of America Chicago Marathon, Boston Art Commission, Boston Athletic Association (BAA), Boston College, the *Boston Globe*, Boston Hotel Buckminster, Boston Public Health Commission, Boston Red Sox, Boston University, Boulder Marathon, Brighton Allston Historical Society, Brookline Historical Society, Church of Saint Ignatius of Loyola, CITGO Petroleum Corporation, the City of Boston, the City of Newton, Framingham Historical Society, General Court of the Commonwealth of Massachusetts

(188th session), Haynes Management Inc., Hopkinton Historical Society, ING New York City Marathon, John Hancock Financial Services, Marathon Run Museum (Greece), Martin W. Richard Charitable Foundation, Massachusetts Bay Community College, Massachusetts Institute of Technology (MIT), Massachusetts Secretary of the Commonwealth Division of Public Records, Massachusetts Trial Court Law Libraries, MetroPCS Dallas Marathon, Natick Historical Society, National Aeronautics and Space Administration (NASA), *New England Runner*, Newton Historical Society, the *New York Times*, the Paul Revere House/Paul Revere Memorial Association, Prudential Center, Running Past, the Sports Museum of New England, St. Jude Memphis Marathon, the Town of Ashland, the Town of Brookline, the Town of Framingham, the Town of Hopkinton, the Town of Marathon (Greece), the Town of Natick, the Town of Wellesley, 26.2 Foundation, USA Track & Field (USATF), Visit Marathon (Greece), Wellesley College, and Wellesley Historical Society.

Also, *The Boston Marathon: A Century of Blood, Sweat, and Cheers* by Tom Derderian; *Boston Marathon: The First Century of the World's Premier Running Event* (Centennial Race Edition) by Tom Derderian; *Boston Marathon Media Guide(s)* by the Boston Athletic Association (BAA) with John Hancock Financial; *Fast Tracks: The History of Distance Running* by Raymond Krise and Bill Squires; and *The Story of the Boston Marathon from 1897* (to 1965) by Jerry Nason and the *Boston Globe*.

INTRODUCTION

B oston.
  That's it. That's all you need. If you're a runner or a fan of running, that one word is all that's required to convey the pinnacle of the sport. The Boston Marathon is considered by many as the ultimate goal—the highest achievement—for a marathoner, especially to those who will never reach the professional ranks or the Olympics.

My connection to the Boston Marathon is manifold. Born and raised less than twenty minutes from the course, I travel over the route on a regular basis and constantly see the landmarks, painted mile and aid station markers that dot the 26.2 miles. For twenty-three consecutive years—from 1990 to 2012—I ran the race on Patriots' Day Monday alongside thousands of fellow marathoners (as a runner, there's no greater feeling than wearing that bib number on your chest).

Since 1988, I have covered the sport of running and the Boston Marathon itself for a variety of media outlets (newspapers, magazines, television) and have interviewed and written about elite racers, amateur runners, and everyone involved in all aspects of the Boston Marathon. Add to that the countless miles of training on the course, and the terrain is forever ingrained in my wiring. In fact, the year I ran Boston for the twenty-third straight time, it had equaled half my life!

Comparatively, I have run nearly twenty other marathons—both out of state and in other countries—and can personally attest that there is no greater experience than Boston. It is truly the jewel of every marathoner's crown. In fact, whenever I am at a marathon other than Boston and people find out where I'm from, I am inevitably bombarded with questions—some as idle interest, others for future use. Either way, it is always exciting and enjoyable to discuss my "home field" marathon.

And that love affair continues. I have spoken of and written about the Boston Marathon for so many years and to so many people that the idea of a book about the course seemed a natural progression. I have obviously come across many books on the subject, and for the most part, they are all good. Really, I'm not kidding! Whether it's a coffee table book, a champion's biography or autobiography, a historical account, a guide on how to qualify, or a collection of essays or photographs—all of them succeed and compose most of my personal running-related library.

When I travel to run a marathon (and also as a fan myself), one of the first things I do is try to find a book on that race. Those that offer the most about the course itself and its history, as well as the locale in which it is run, are the most enjoyable and rewarding.

And that's where this book comes in.

Nowhere else does one book on the Boston Marathon feature everything that I look for—and offer—in a single title. From a twenty-three-year Boston Marathon veteran, there are detailed course descriptions; unique, fun, and interesting facts, anecdotes, and historical insights on the cities and towns, the race, and the course itself; vintage photographs and original and distinctive runner-perspective pictures; useful and entertaining observations and overviews; and exclusive expert course-specific advice.

Regarding that last aspect, of particular interest is the featured wisdom from Notre Dame All-American and 1980 U.S. Olympic 10K/marathon coach Bill Squires, the renowned former coach of the fabled Greater Boston Track Club (GBTC), which began in 1973 at Boston College and whose training ground includes the Boston Marathon roads, especially the Newton hills.

Whether through GBTC or on his own, Squires coached athletes who went on to win a phenomenal eight Boston Marathon titles from 1975 to 1983, including national push-rim wheelchair champion Bob Hall (1975, 1977), Bill Rodgers (1975, 1978–80), Alberto Salazar (1982), and Greg Meyer (1983); earned fifteen non-winning top-ten finishes in 1977 (Vinnie Fleming in fifth), 1978 (Jeff Wells in second, Jack Fultz in fourth, Randy Thomas in fifth), 1979 (Bob Hodge in third, Thomas in eighth, Dick Mahoney in tenth), 1980 (Kevin Ryan in ninth, Mike Pinocci in tenth), 1981 (Rodgers in third, John Lodwick in fourth), 1982 (Dick Beardsley in second, Lodwick in third, Rodgers in

Bill Squires, legendary coach of the Greater Boston Track Club, coached some of the greats in the sport, including Boston Marathon winners Bill Rodgers, Alberto Salazar, Greg Meyer, and wheelchair champion Bob Hall. *Courtesy Jack McDonald.*

fourth), and 1983 (Rodgers in tenth); and won back-to-back team titles in 1978 (Rodgers, Fultz, Thomas) and 1979 (Rodgers, Hodge, Thomas) and a third-place team finish in 1975 (Rodgers, Scott Graham, Vinnie Fleming).

In addition, within a nearly forty-year span, Squires ran the Boston Marathon several times, most notably in 1961, when he came in twentieth with a time of 2:47:46. He has also combed over, measured, and analyzed every inch of the course, including painting mile markers in the early days (before mile markers were painted) and performing his tangent-slope experiment of monitoring the path of a rolling tennis ball down a tricky portion of the course to determine the line of least resistance for his athletes. And for nearly fifteen years as part of the John Hancock Running and Fitness Program, through various sessions and course tours, he guided countless

Shown in the 1984 U.S. Olympic Trials Marathon are Boston Marathon champions (from left) Greg Meyer (1983), Alberto Salazar (1982), and Bill Rodgers (1975, 1978–80). *Photo by Leo Kulinski Jr.*

runners and several contemporary foreign champions. Needless to say, he knows of what he speaks.

So, enjoy this ride over 26.2 miles/42.195 kilometers of sacred and cherished pavement. Whether sitting comfortably at home during the training for Boston, on the plane en route to the Bay State, in a Boston hotel awaiting the nerves to calm, or simply as a fan of the sport anywhere in the world, I hope this book provides the necessary entertainment, advice, fun, and escape.

Are you ready? On your mark, get set…

CHAPTER 1

THE BOSTON MARATHON

Like most great things in life, the Boston Marathon in its current form of nearly thirty thousand participants began humbly enough, with but fifteen men.

Thanks to a handful of members of the nine-year-old Boston Athletic Association (BAA) who competed in and witnessed the beautiful and otherworldly 1896 Modern Olympic Games in Athens, Greece, a spark was kindled that remained burning on their return home to America. Of the dozen men-only events at the Games, the marathon, in particular, so struck John Graham, the club's coach/manager, that the seed was planted for what would become the grand dame of marathons.

The marathon is modeled after the accepted mythological story of ancient Greek soldier and messenger Pheidippides, who after a twenty-four-mile run from the battlegrounds of Marathon to the city of Athens in 490 BC to report the Athenian victory over the superior Persian forces, proclaimed, "Nenikekamen!" ("We have won!") and instantly succumbed to a heroic death. Despite the historically and factually combined legend, the amalgamation survived to inspire millions. So much so that the word itself—marathon—has become known as more than a town in Greece; it is the pinnacle of duration, a far cry from its root origin as that of the flowered plant marathos (known as fennel) from that region of the world.

The first marathon footrace was held on March 10, 1896, in Greece and served as an ancient "qualifier" for the Modern Olympic Games marathon one month later, on April 10, 1896. Fittingly, the hometown

Greeks won both races—Kharilaos Vasilakos in its debut and Spyridon Louis in the Olympics.

At the time in the United States, the BAA held its own multi-event competition called, simply enough, the BAA Games. From the Olympics, Graham had brought with him the embryonic idea and plans that would become the closing event of the BAA Games on April 19, 1897. According to the BAA, it was known in its infancy by several names, including the American Marathon, the BAA Road Race, and the BAA Marathon. And much like the 1896 Olympic Marathon was the second one held, so, too, was Boston's in the United States. About six months prior to the BAA's race, there had been a marathon that ran from Stamford, Connecticut, to the Knickerbocker Athletic Club at the Columbia Circle Oval in New York City. Interestingly, the victor of both U.S. marathons was John J. McDermott of New York.

To create the new course that approximated the Greek distance of about forty kilometers (24.85 miles), it was initially thought to follow in reverse order the route of Paul Revere's famous Midnight Ride of April 18–19, 1775, to warn of the British soldiers who were on their way to arrest soon-to-be president of the Continental Congress John Hancock and future Massachusetts governor Samuel Adams. Revere's ride, which took him from Charlestown to Boston (via the Charles River by boat) and then through Somerville (part of Charlestown back then), Medford (Mistick back then), and Lexington (where he was joined by fellow rider William Dawes via his separate route), was 13.25 miles.

Add to that distance Revere's extra journey with Dawes (and then also with Dr. Samuel Prescott) of their own volition toward Concord, and the route increased 3.20 miles to the point where they were stopped by British soldiers in Lincoln and Revere was captured. In the end, the overall mileage was 16.45 miles, according to historian Charles Bahne and the Paul Revere House/Paul Revere Memorial Association. The BAA's forefathers would have undoubtedly added on the necessary 8.00 or so miles, but 122 years of institutional memory loss and landscape and roadway changes appeared to have proved the original route too difficult to replicate.

Alternately, an approximate clockwise radius of the marathon distance to the north of Boston is just beyond the town of Lawrence and closes in on the New Hampshire state line. To the east is the Massachusetts Bay, to the south is just beyond the town of Mansfield and near the Rhode Island state line, and to the west is Ashland, through which traveled the Boston and Albany Railroad line. Home to such accommodating access, Ashland

With bicyclists leading the way, and a few waiting on the sidewalk at right, the field of the third annual Boston Marathon in 1899 makes its way up the dirt road of Main Street in Ashland. *Courtesy Ashland Historical Society*.

played host to the Boston Marathon for its first twenty-seven years and included three separate start locations. Hopkinton, the neighboring town to the west, has been the host town since 1924 and also included several different start lines.

The distance of the Boston Marathon has fluctuated over the many decades, and not always by design—well, perhaps at times by design, but not always on purpose. The first twenty-seven runnings of the race landed in proximity to the 40K distance—in the vicinity of 24.0 to 25.0 miles, but most of them at 24.5 miles.

For the 1908 Games of the IV Olympiad in London, England, the marathon distance was extended to 26 miles and 385 yards (42.195 kilometers) to include a Windsor Castle start and an alternative track finish in front of the royal family box inside the Olympic White City Stadium.

While many marathoners' anger since then has been justifiably aimed toward then-reigning King Edward VII, Queen Alexandra, and the Royal family for this additional footage, especially when struggling over the last couple miles, often forgotten is the fact that the 1908 Olympic Games were originally scheduled to be hosted by Rome but were relocated to the

United Kingdom after the fatal 1906 Mount Vesuvius volcano eruption that decimated Naples (national focus turned from hosting the Games to rebuilding the city). Had those Olympic Games been held in Rome, who knows what distance the marathon would have become.

Thanks in large part to the nonprofit 26.2 Foundation (formerly the Hopkinton Athletic Association), the connection between the Olympic Marathon in Greece and the Boston Marathon can be seen in many ways.

The most constant nod is the laurel wreaths that are bestowed upon the male and female winners. The wreaths, which are fashioned from olive branches in the Greek town of Marathon, travel to Boston, where a ceremony takes place between the city's Greek consulate general and Boston Marathon race officials. Replacing the previous chase-down approach at the finish line to place it on the (often still moving) winner of the old days is the current means of a more respectable laying of the wreath on the winner's head at the finish-line awards podium. That ceremony also features the medal presentation and the playing of the winners' national anthems, of which there are 140 different recordings at the ready.

On the High Street bridge in Ashland, which was the second start-line location in Boston Marathon history, participants of the 1906 race gather before the tenth running. *Courtesy Ashland Historical Society.*

In addition, special gold, silver, and bronze wreaths are also donated by Dimitri Kyriakides, the son of 1947 Boston Marathon winner Stylianos Kyriakides, whose run and subsequent victory brought attention and much-needed food and supplies to his post–World War II homeland.

Also in recognition of the Boston Marathon's link to the 1896 Olympic Marathon was the Flame of the Marathon Run. In 2008, a specially built cauldron on Hopkinton Town Common was lit with a flame that originated from the warriors' tomb in Marathon. The Flame of the Marathon Run burned brightly during the 112th Boston Marathon and was later used to light a ceremonious light post outside the Hopkinton Police Department.

In regard to the marathon's change to 26.2 miles in 1908, the BAA responded sixteen years later for its 1924 edition, stretching out the distance accordingly. Or so it thought. While the Boston Marathon from 1924 to 1926 was understood to be the standard distance, a remeasurement of the course in 1927 revealed that the distance fell short by 197 yards, meaning that the previous three runs were 26.0 miles, 209 yards. All was well—and at 26.2 miles—from 1927 until 1950. Then, due to unmeasured road construction and reconfigurations along the course unrelated to the race, the Boston Marathon from 1951 to 1956 was 25.0 miles, 1,232 yards. Since 1957, the race has been 26.2 miles.

Other than short portions on Chestnut Hill Avenue, Hereford Street, and Boylston Street, the point-to-point course of the Boston Marathon is composed of five routes: Route 135 from the start to Wellesley; Route 16 from Wellesley to Newton; Route 30 from West Newton to Brighton and, later, in Boston and Kenmore Square; Route 9A from Brookline to Boston; and Route 2 in Boston.

Another unique staple of the race is that it is held on the Patriots' Day holiday, which has simultaneously remained constant while also having often changed. The first race (Monday, April 19, 1897) was held on the four-year-old holiday that commemorated the 1775 battles in the towns of Lexington and Concord that began the Revolutionary War, Paul Revere's Midnight Ride, and other Massachusetts observances.

For the first seventy-two years, the Boston Marathon was run on April 19 unless that was a Sunday (with two exceptions due to World War II). Since 1969, when Patriots' Day was designated as the third Monday in April, the Boston Marathon has been held on that fixed day, which is also known colloquially as Marathon Monday.

One other unique mainstay of the Boston Marathon has been its start time, which for over one hundred years was at noon. The first major time change occurred in 2004, when the elite women had their own start at 11:31 a.m., followed by the regular noontime gun for the rest of the field. In 2006, a two-wave start was added as the first ten thousand runners started at noon and the rest at 12:30 p.m. The following year saw an even greater change to the start time when the gun was fired at 10:00 a.m.

The current schedule features multiple starts for the mobility impaired at 9:00 a.m., the push-rim wheelchair division at 9:17 a.m., handcycle athletes at 9:22 a.m., elite women at 9:32 a.m., elite men and the first wave of men and women at 10:00 a.m., a second wave at 10:20 a.m., and a third wave at 10:40 a.m.

Regarding official female entrants, there were none for the first seventy-five years. It wasn't until the 1972 Boston Marathon, when the governing body Amateur Athletic Union (AAU) included an addendum in its rules handbook, that women could officially run that distance. Nina Kuscsik of New York won in a course-record (CR) time of 3:10:26.

Within the ensuing eleven years, female winners set two world records (WR) at the Boston Marathon—Liane Winter of West Germany in 1975 (2:42:24) and Joan Benoit Samuelson of Maine in 1983 (2:22:43)—doubling the number set by the men's overall winners, as only Yun Bok Suh of Korea set a WR 2:25:39 in 1947 (John Campbell of New Zealand also set a WR with a 2:11:04 in 1990 in the men's masters division).

Women also outnumber the men three to one in regard to Olympic Marathon gold medalists who have also won Boston: Benoit Samuelson (1979 and 1983 Bostons; 1984 Olympics), Rosa Mota of Portugal (1987, 1988, 1990 Bostons; 1988 Olympics), and Fatuma Roba of Ethiopia (1997, 1998, 1999 Bostons; 1996 Olympics). To date, Gelindo Bordin of Italy is the only men's Boston winner (1990) who also won Olympic Marathon gold (1988).

The AAU's tardiness did not mean women never ran the Boston Marathon prior to 1972, of course. Eight different women (some in multiple years) ran between 1966 and 1971, and the BAA has since recognized Roberta "Bobbi" Gibb of Massachusetts/California (1966, 1967, 1968) and Sara Mae Berman of Massachusetts (1969, 1970, 1971) as champions of those years.

Canadian Jacqueline Gareau won the 1980 Boston Marathon but had to wait a week for her wreath and accolades after an investigation concluded that Rosie Ruiz, the first woman to cross the finish line, had cheated. *Photo by Leo Kulinski Jr.*

In 1975, the Boston Marathon officially included a wheelchair division when Bob Hall finished in 2:58:00, two minutes under the three-hour limit race director William "Will" Cloney set for Hall to reach in order to receive an official certificate and be officially recognized. This was five years after Eugene Roberts of Maryland had completed the 1970 Boston Marathon in about seven hours sans an official bib number.

The Boston Marathon wheelchair division race in 1977 also doubled as the National Wheelchair Championships, which Hall won. In 1984, the race was officially sanctioned by the BAA, and prize money was added for the first time in 1986. To date, it has recorded fourteen men's WRs and eleven women's WRs.

There were also three instances in which the top two women's finish times were identical (winners Louise Sauvage of Australia in 1998 and 1999 and Christina Ripp of Illinois in 2003) and two one-second victories (winners Masazumi Soejima of Japan in 2011 and Shirley Reilly of Arizona in 2012).

Then there's the relationship between the Boston Marathon fields and qualifying standards. For the first seventy-three years, men who could run

The Boston Marathon is the first major marathon to feature a division for wheelchair athletes. Current fields in the dozens line up in Hopkinton, as shown here in 1998. *Courtesy New England Runner.*

the marathon distance—and, in later years, who could also pass an on-site physical and the muster test administered by race official and staunch gatekeeper John "Jock" Semple—were allowed to compete.

In 1970, a four-hour qualification certification was required, followed in the ensuing years by several recalculations and stringent age-group standards that were all initially instituted to weed out the unqualified non-athletes and maintain the field. But it all ended up creating an ultimate and exclusive goal that subsequently increased interest and participation. And when field limits capped bib numbers, the Boston Marathon truly became the treasured golden ring.

According to the BBA, including the 2013 race, there have been more than half a million entrants since its inception—550,436, to be precise. From 18 entrants in its first year to a record peak of 38,708 in its 100th in 1996, it took ten years before there were more than 100 entrants for Boston (105 in 1906) and seventy-two years before an entrant field cracked 1,000 (1,014 in 1968).

The running boom of the 1970s provided steady growth in the thousands, with peaks of 9,629 in 1992 and 9,416 in 1995. And after the record centennial field in 1996, and a yearly average of 14,000 from 1997 to 2002, entrant numbers since 2003 have averaged 24,000 a year, with a steady annual range of over 26,000 since 2009.

The Boston Marathon in the early to mid-1980s experienced severe growing pains on its way to an eventual transformation that was imperative for its survival. Decades after the eight-bit entrance fee and the days when a couple people could handle the mailed-in applications and house the dollar bills in a single envelope in a safe, running and marathons were starting to become big business—moneymakers for cities and organizations, as well as top athletes.

When the lock on pure amateurism began to crack, and young and new major-city marathons began to open their financial doors to welcome international elite athletes with appearance fees, transportation, boarding, etc.—among other decision-making foresight—the Boston Marathon's early response was to maintain its traditions to the point of the exclusion of any growth.

However, a near-fatal attempt to procure answers and sponsors occurred within an unsettling four-year span between 1980 and 1984.

According to public documents found in the Massachusetts Trial Court Law Libraries, late in 1980, Will Cloney, the BAA president and board of governor member, began to meet with Marshall Medoff, a local Boston attorney, with the intention of attracting to the race better promotion and sponsorship to ensure its future. In April 1981, Cloney, by vote of the board, was granted authority to "negotiate" and "execute" in regard to the obtainment of funds all agreed were needed to provide life to the race. Cloney, on his own, again met with Medoff and by September 1981 had signed over rights to Medoff and his newly created sports promotion company, International Marathons Inc. (IMI).

In February 1982, five months after the deal had been made, the BAA learned of the terms, which included the provision that the BAA could not enter into an agreement with a sponsor without first consulting IMI and that it would receive an annual cap of $400,000, with any overage to be paid to IMI. It also learned of the agreement's open-ended potential of annually renewing itself. The board voted in September of that year that it was beyond the authority of Cloney to agree to such terms without first presenting them to the board.

Subsequently, the BAA filed a lawsuit against IMI (and others). In July 1984, after nearly two years of injunctions, motions, and court proceedings, the agreement was declared "void and unenforceable," largely due to neither the nonprofit BAA board having the authority to

When John Hancock Mutual Life Insurance Company joined as the principal sponsor of the Boston Marathon and began to award prize money, the race attracted large and fast international fields, such as in 1987, when there were ten countries represented in the top ten men's and women's finishes. *Photo by Leo Kulinski Jr.*

empower Cloney nor Cloney having the sole authority to commit to such an agreement.

Shortly thereafter, in 1985, the local John Hancock Mutual Life Insurance Company signed a multi-year principal sponsorship deal (which John Hancock Financial Services has renewed many times over). As a result, the 1986 Boston Marathon was the first one in its ninety-year history to award prize money, of which the world took notice and showed up to compete. Almost immediately, exciting matchups, close finishes, and competitors from numerous countries began to add to the race's legacy.

While there had obviously been foreign winners at the Boston Marathon prior to the John Hancock sponsorship, that 1986 race featured seven different countries represented within the top ten men and eight countries within the top ten women.

Australia's Robert de Castella won the Boston Marathon in 1986, the first year prize money was awarded. *Victah Sailer photo courtesy* New England Runner.

Regarding race directors of the Boston Marathon, there have been only four. Well, technically only four. For the first fifty years, the marathon was run and organized by a committee, with various people heading the many areas of concern. For many years, race official Semple, primarily the physical

In 1969, Boston Arena manager Paul V. Brown (right) stepped in to continue the then-sixty-five-year-old Brown family tradition of starting the Boston Marathon. *Courtesy Tom Burke.*

therapist and trainer for the Boston Bruins of the NHL and the Boston Celtics of the NBA, could fit any and all paperwork, applications, fees, etc., in his rubdown "office" inside the old Boston Garden.

It wasn't until Cloney in 1947 that there was an official race director. He remained the race director for thirty-six years and was followed by Tim Kilduff (1983–84), Guy Morse III (1985–2000), and Dave McGillivray, who started in 2001.

There is also a deep, longtime, wide-ranging military connection to the Boston Marathon. Due to World War I, the 1918 race was a ten-man military relay held on Friday, April 19. It was won by the Camp Devens Divisional Team from the Bay State town of Ayer, followed in second place by the 302nd Infantry, Camp Devens, and in third by the Boston Navy Yard. And starting in 2005, there has been—with the proper signage and medals provided by the BAA—a Boston Marathon run overseas. Locations have included Camp Adder Ali Air Base in Talil, Iraq; the USS *Nimitz* (CVN-68) aircraft carrier; and Bagram Airfield in the Parwan Province in Afghanistan.

And aboard the International Space Station (ISS), Expedition 14 flight engineer Sunita "Suni" Williams of Massachusetts, a NASA astronaut who had qualified for Boston, was tethered to a treadmill and traveled five miles per second when she finished the 2007 Boston Marathon some 210 miles above the course in a time of 4:23:10. Later, on the actual terra firma of the Boston Marathon, she steadily improved on her time in 2008 (4:20:42) and 2009 (3:49:49).

Weather-wise, April in New England runs the gamut. The race has featured sleet (1907), snow (1908, 1925), snow squalls (1961, 1967), and mist so dense that it prevented helicopters from flying to provide the usual wire-to-wire television coverage (2002). Rain has also pelted the runners, most notably in 2007, when a strong wind-swept-rain nor'easter prompted nearly 2,500 bib numbers to go unclaimed and the elephant-in-the-room possibility of cancellation to linger into the early morning hours on race day. And while a storm also blocked the sun for the 1939 Boston Marathon, it was primarily due to a partial solar eclipse that darkened the skies at the start.

While it is rare for a marathon to be cancelled or stopped due to Mother Nature (Boston came close in 2007), it does occur. Fatal heat in October 2007 prompted Bank of America Chicago Marathon organizers to prematurely stop the race in response to the growing number of runners who were succumbing to the climbing temperatures. In 2012, the devastating aftermath of deadly Hurricane Sandy in November forced the ING New York City Marathon to be cancelled. And in 2013, September's Boulder Marathon was postponed until the fall of 2014 due to a historic deadly flood, while severe December ice storms caused the cancellation of both the St. Jude Memphis Marathon (the location of which was in a state of emergency) and the MetroPCS Dallas Marathon.

The most common weather-related foe for runners, of course, is the heat. While the Boston Marathon has experienced many years in the '70s and '80s that were most uncomfortable and potentially dangerous to the participants, there was extreme heat in 1905 (one hundred degrees), the 1909 "Inferno" (ninety-seven degrees), 1927 (eighty-four degrees, which promptly melted newly paved portions of the course), the "Run for the Hoses" in 1976 (ninety-six degrees), 2004 (eighty-six degrees) and 2012 (eighty-nine degrees), the last of which elicited the BAA to take unprecedented measures. Less than five years after the 2007 Chicago Marathon stoppage, Boston Marathon officials—powered by the consistent forecasts for a hot race day—prior to the race had offered official runners the opportunity to defer their 2012 entries to 2013. The BAA also extended its official course time from six hours to seven hours to afford runners more time to finish safely and not feel compelled to push themselves into danger (although, as the day and temps grew, so, too, did the time limit).

All along the course, the towns and cities and their inhabitants roll out the welcome mat for the world and dress up the streets and environs that ensure and capture the exuberance and excitement that is the Boston Marathon.

Residents decorate their homes and lawns with makeshift getups that attract attention, including one Natick family in particular who always feature an interesting front-yard structure from which people watch the race; various signs of encouragement—and humor—including an Entering Boston sign within the first few miles; all-day family barbecues; inspirational music blaring from windows and garages; and bands rockin' all day from various driveways.

So connected are the town and city residents along the course that oftentimes the same people look forward to the runners and offer drinks, ice cubes, candy, bottled water, wet sponges, and towels. And for several years in Hopkinton, where many residents open their homes to runners, a woman brought homemade cookies and brownies for the media personnel who would begin their live reports at the start line in the darkness of the early morning hours.

Weeks—and sometimes months—out from Patriots' Day, the various public works departments along the route begin sprucing up their special portions of the course. Potholes are filled, road hazards are tended to, traffic islands and town commons are landscaped, and everything receives a fresh paintjob.

Banners and bunting are hung with great care. Also, about a month before the race, four-time Boston Marathon winner Bill Rodgers climbs aboard a cherry picker in downtown Boston and unveils one of the hundreds of Marathon banners to the applause and delight of fans, onlookers, spectators, and news media. And course-specific markers—miles, kilometers, aid stations, etc.—are reapplied.

In the earlier years, checkpoints were located at such odd distances as 2.4 miles in Ashland; 4.75 miles, 6.50 miles, 6.75 miles in Framingham; 9.50 miles, 10.25 miles, 10.50 miles in Natick; 13.25 miles, 13.50 miles, 13.75 miles in Wellesley; 17.50 miles, 17.75 miles in Newton; 21.50 miles, 24.12 miles, 24.30 miles in Brookline—all dependent upon the start location. This was not for the runners but due in large part to the nearest means of transportation for the race officials.

"I'll clue ya," legendary coach Bill Squires says with some envy of the uniform checkpoint mile markers, "enjoy them. In the old days, they had about four. Five, tops! Seventeen was near the fire station. And the one at 9.5 would be at the armory near 10.0 miles when it was cold or raining because they [race officials] could stay inside to get warm. And each of the markers were wooden horses—sandwich boards—and every year someone would bring them and watch them because someone stole them one time."

And in the weeks and days leading up to Marathon Monday, local and area newspapers highlight the many stories of their own participating residents. Daily newspapers feature articles about the painting of the start and finish lines, special commemorative ceremonies, the incoming field of elite athletes, and the inevitable predictions.

Local and national television news programs air months-long stories on runners they've followed during training, while businesses, hotels, restaurants, and vendors decorate their storefronts and kiosks with everything running related. Hopkinton police officers even hold up traffic at the start line so visitors can snap pictures of themselves at the famous site on Route 135.

The charitable element of the Boston Marathon has also blossomed into a multimillion-dollar success story that has attracted thousands of participants who have raised much-needed funds for dozens of organizations.

In 1986, when John Hancock Mutual Life Insurance Company became the principal sponsor of the race, it also began the John Hancock Non-Profit Program, which designates a select number of charities—in addition to interested John Hancock Financial Services and Manulife employees—to receive official bib numbers to raise funds. In its first twenty-eight years, the program has raised more than $30 million, including a record $7.8 million during the 2013 Boston Marathon.

In 1989, when the American Liver Foundation received from the BAA official bib numbers without the need to qualify, the Boston Marathon Charity Program was born. It has since grown to include an average of thirty selected organizations that receive official bib numbers as an active means to raise money. More than $140 million has been raised in its first twenty-five years.

There is no escaping the Boston Marathon. And for good reason. In addition to the natural pride involved, the influx of 27,000-plus entrants; nearly 100,000 visitors to the three-day expo; 14,000 volunteers, medical, security, police, and officials; over 1,000 media personnel (second only to the Super Bowl); and more than 500,000 spectators, the Boston Marathon boosts the local economy by an average of $132 million (estimates according to the BAA's 2013 numbers).

In 2006, the World Marathon Majors Series was created with the Boston Marathon, the Virgin London Marathon, the real-Berlin Marathon, the Bank of America Chicago Marathon, and the ING New York City Marathon (the Tokyo Marathon joined in 2012). A top-five point system tallied over a two-year span of these qualifying marathons—and the IAAF (International Association of Athletics Federations) World Championships Marathon and

Olympic Marathon—provide elite athletes the chance to compete for series prize money.

The growth of the Boston Marathon has been phenomenal. What began with a handful of runners and officials on dirt roads has turned into a race of tens of thousands over finely surfaced pavement. The humble post-race "winnings" of a medal, trophies, and beef stew has grown to include hundreds of thousands of dollars (minus the beef stew).

And the Boston Marathon has also expanded to not only being a race on its own but also, on occasion, a select championship.

The thirty-first annual Boston Marathon also served as the 1927 AAU Marathon Championship, won by Clarence DeMar of Massachusetts. In his fifth of seven Boston crowns, DeMar also set a CR with a time of 2:40:22.

In 2007, the 111th Boston Marathon was also the U.S. Women's Marathon Championship for the first time in its history. Deena Kastor of California won in a time of 2:35:09.

One day before the 112th Boston Marathon was held the 2008 U.S. Olympic Team Trials Women's Marathon, the course of which was a multi-lap route through Boston and Cambridge that also used the finish line of the Boston Marathon. The Olympic team was composed of the top three finishers: Kastor in first (2:29:35), Magdalena Lewy Boulet of California in second (2:30:19), and Blake Russell of California in third (2:32:40).

The following year—2009—introduced a number of additions to Boston Marathon Weekend when, on the day before the marathon, the BAA held its first annual BAA 5K. This race soon became part of the BAA Distance Medley race series, which consists of the BAA 5K (April), the BAA 10K (June), and the BAA Half-Marathon (October). And along with the BAA 5K on Sunday is the BAA Invitational Mile races (men and women) and BAA Scholastic Invitational Mile races (high school boys and girls), all utilizing the finish line on Boylston Street.

The BAA 5K and invitational mile races are in addition to an already packed weekend of running. Since 1997, hundreds of kids from community youth clubs compete in the BAA Relay Challenge on Boylston Street as part of a four-week training and running program that ends with this event. Categories include age groups and teams.

The scope and magnitude of the Boston Marathon can also be measured in the supplies alone, which tell part of the story. According to the BAA, items used for the 2013 Boston Marathon included the following: more than sixty thousand feet of rope, fifty thousand feet of cable, thirty thousand feet of fencing, ten thousand trash bags, two thousand tables, 1.4 million paper cups, 108,000 safety pins, one thousand portable toilets, forty thousand

Heatsheet blankets, twenty-seven thousand race shirts, twenty-seven thousand participant bags, and twenty-seven thousand medals.

The numbers for the pre-race pasta party, held the evening before the Boston Marathon and so large that it takes several seatings on the Government Center grounds of Boston City Hall, are equally staggering: 11,300 pounds of pasta, nearly three thousand quarts of tomato sauce, 3,400 pounds of fresh vegetables, seventeen thousand cups of coffee and tea, thirty-five thousand gallons of water, 140 wait staff and chefs, and more than five thousand hours of prep work and cooking.

The medical setup at the start, along the course, and at the finish is a fine-tuned process designed to handle most emergencies, as expertly proven in 2013 in response to the bombings on Boylston.

There are a total of thirty American Red Cross stations—two at the Athletes' Village near the start, twenty-six on the course, and two at the finish area—in addition to several medical sweep buses that stop at various aid stations along the course.

Nearly 330 medical volunteers put in two thousand combined hours to assist runners and spectators who require attention, which on average range between 1,000 and 2,000 people per year. Communication is also managed by 120 ham-radio operators.

Some of the medical supplies at the start and finish include, on average, twenty-five electrocardiogram (EKG) machines, forty defibrillators, 150 blood pressure cuffs and stethoscopes, eighty thermometers, five hundred bags of ice, 380 cots, 1,500 blankets, four thousand Band-Aids, twenty-six oxygen tanks, nine hundred intravenous (IV) bags, five hundred sick bags, five hundred tongue depressors, and two thousand adhesive bandages.

Along the course there is an average of more than thirty boxes of gloves, fifty bottles of sunblock lotion, five thousand Band-Aids, 250 ice packs, fifty-two heat packs, 150 pounds of petroleum jelly, and 1,500 gauze pads.

Over 14,000 race officials, volunteers, medical and emergency personnel, and security officers are charged with the responsibility of ensuring the overall safety and enjoyment of the 27,000 runners and 500,000 spectators in the eight cities and towns on more than twenty-six miles of roadway for approximately twelve hours (and more)—from before the first runner arrives at the Athletes' Village until the last one passes through the finish-line area.

Recognized and respected as the oldest annually contested marathon in the world, the Boston Marathon reaches millions of people in more than two hundred countries through the media. According to the BAA, on average, nearly 1,100 media credentials are issued to 180 outlets, eighty print publications, thirty-six television and radio stations, and ten news agencies, which reach daily and weekly newspapers, magazines, and television and radio programs, and various online media worldwide.

Between the BAA and others, the Boston Marathon course is closely monitored by a variety of means for a number of reasons, some of which include safety, security, timing, race results, emergencies, etc. The BAA has several electronic and manual checkpoints, as well as countless volunteers, officials, video, and pictures covering the entire course.

From newspaper to radio and television coverage, the Boston Marathon has been subject to much media in its history. At its peak, radio stations competed for the best information from those on the course who were following the action. For newspapers, the city of Boston offered numerous daily editions from several outlets. And on the small screen, early tape-delay coverage evolved into marketing battles and heated ratings wars between multiple stations. All of this has increased the notoriety and popularity of the sport, the event, and the athletes.

As for the live wire-to-wire local television coverage, the Spotters Network—an entity separate from the BAA that was co-founded by Fred Treseler and Tim Kilduff and provides instantaneous race-day data collection and distribution from the course—is an elaborate mechanism of volunteers along the route who, using an intricate process, spot the leaders, record them passing by specific marks, and instantaneously communicate the splits and other relevant data to the television studio.

A bank of additional trained volunteers then conveys said information to the on-air anchors (they also receive streams of lead-vehicle commentary), who are continuously covering the four separately timed races—wheelchair men, wheelchair women, men's open, and women's open—in such a way that the viewer at home is provided with the utmost current details possible.

There are also thirty-six digital timer clocks—including one at each mile and every 5K mark—that coincide with the 10:00 a.m. start. And every mile and 5K mark are so designated with official signage.

For so many reasons, the Boston Marathon has become the measuring stick for the sport. No other marathon outside the Olympics possesses such pull for anyone who calls him or herself a marathoner, from the elites to the middle-of-the-packers to those in the back.

The Boston Marathon is on many a runner's bucket list, whether attainable or not. For a fan, the Boston Marathon is an exceptional competitive (with the elites) and inspirational (with the non-elites) event. And for the spectator, the Boston Marathon is the ultimate communal gathering.

CHAPTER 2

HOPKINTON:
MILES 0.00 TO 1.90

I t all starts here!" That's what the familiar sign on Hopkinton Town Common announces with pride. And it is true, of course—since 1924.

The first twenty-seven starts of the Boston Marathon began in the border town of Ashland. To align itself with the newly accepted Olympic marathon distance of 26 miles and 385 yards, the BAA traveled west along West Union Street in Ashland to East Main Street until the new distance was reached in Hopkinton.

The roots of the town's name stem from seven-term Connecticut Colony governor Edward Hopkins, who upon his death in 1657 in England—119 years before the Declaration of Independence—left in his will a posthumous gift to Harvard College that afforded the university the ability to buy land that would become Hopkinstown and, eventually, Hopkinton. Established in 1715, the town of 18,500 acres also was composed of Ashland and portions of the towns of Holliston and Upton.

On average, every third Monday in April, the town's population of just under fifteen thousand balloons to nearly forty thousand runners, spectators, volunteers, media, officials, etc. Yet within hours after the marathon participants exit on their way to Boston, Hopkinton somehow returns to relative normalcy, save for the sight of an occasional police fence and orange highway barrel.

Unlike most major-city marathons, the Boston Marathon starts in a town a third its size and on less than two miles of roadway. Runners spend more time on the bus en route to Hopkinton, in the Athletes' Village, or even in the corrals than they do running the first 1.90 miles to the next town.

The always beautifully painted Jacques "Jack" LeDuc start line of the Boston Marathon. *Photo by Paul C. Clerici.*

Despite the onslaught of humanity, Hopkinton is extremely welcoming of its part-time visitors (this is a common trait evidenced by the manner in which the Hopkinton Board of Selectmen greets each new homeowner/ resident to town with a welcome letter that also apprises them of town services, volunteer opportunities, etc.). In the days and weeks leading up to Patriots' Day Monday, the town decorates itself with colorful banners and signs that embrace the race. Stores and households drape greetings of good luck and well wishes for the runners, and roads, landscapes, and public ways are freshened up and polished for the big day.

One of those pavement accents is courtesy of Jacques "Jack" LeDuc of Ashland, who applies his artistic talents to East Main Street. A few days prior to the Marathon, LeDuc, on his hands and knees and with police protection from traffic, paints the thirty-nine-foot-long colorful start line, a job he enjoys with his assistants, who happen to be his daughters, Jeannie Bloom and Laura McGee.

A closer look at the start-line artwork each year reveals hidden (and not-so hidden) messages and remembrances, such as an ocean wave from curb to curb to mark the first year of the wave starts; faux tire tracks that mimicked real ones that are often left by vehicles; a large runner's bib number "40" to commemorate the fortieth anniversary of the first official women's start; and initials or images of those associated with the race who have passed away.

Also within a few days of the race—with the steady dominance of the Kenyan runners, whose men have won the Boston Marathon twenty times between 1988 and 2013 (including an unparalleled string of ten in a row from 1991 to 2000) and whose countrywomen have won all but four between 2000 and 2013—the Elmwood Elementary School in Hopkinton plays host to the John Hancock Scholars and Stars program, where a visit by the elite African runners culminates weeks of Kenya-specific cultural and environmental study and learning by the students. And this is by no means a stagnant entrance. To the vocal exuberance of several hundred cheering students in the darkened school gym, the athletes' rock-star intro is bathed in dry ice, colorful nightclub-style lights, and invigorating music as they jog in and low-five the seated kids.

Regarding multiple winners, there have been sixteen in the men's open, seven in the women's open, eight in the men's wheelchair division, and seven in the women's wheelchair division.

Leading the way is Ernst Van Dyk of South Africa in the men's wheelchair with a remarkable nine titles, followed by Jean Driscoll of Illinois in the women's wheelchair with eight, Clarence DeMar in the men's open with seven, Candace Cable-Brookes in the women's wheelchair with six, Jim Knaub of California in the men's wheelchair with five, and Wakako Tsuchida of Japan in the women's wheelchair with five.

Four-time winners include Robert Kipkoech Cheruiyot of Kenya, Gerard Cote of Canada, and Bill Rodgers in the men's open; Catherine Ndereba of Kenya in the women's open; and Louise Sauvage in the women's wheelchair.

Three-time winners include Ibrahim Hussein of Kenya, Comsas Ndeti of Kenya, Eino Oksanen of Finland, and Leslie "Les" Pawson of Rhode Island in the men's open; Rosa Mota, Uta Pippig of Germany, and Fatuma Roba in the women's open (with Bobbi Gibb and Sara Mae Berman); and Andre Viger of Canada in the men's wheelchair.

And two-time winners include Ellison "Tarzan" Brown of Rhode Island, John P. Caffery of Canada, Johnny "The Elder" Kelley of Massachusetts, Johnny Miles of Canada, Toshihiko Seko of Japan, Geoff Smith of Great Britain, Moses Tanui of Kenya, and Aurele Vandendriessche of Belgium in the men's open; Michiko "Miki" Gorman of California, Ingrid Kristiansen of Norway, and Joan Benoit Samuelson in the women's open; Heinz Frei of Switzerland, Bob Hall, George Murray of Florida, and Masazumi Soejima

Three-peat (1994–96) Boston Marathon champion Uta Pippig of Germany runs through Framingham in 1995 with Maine Running Hall of Fame member Paul Hammond (242) on her heels. *Bill Boyle photo courtesy* New England Runner.

A sea of runners makes its way through some of the winding miles of the Boston Marathon course. *Jonathan S. McElvery photo courtesy* New England Runner.

The simply stated one-mile marker in 1984 lacks the current colorful signage and manpower as Geoff Smith of Great Britain takes the early lead in the first of his back-to-back Boston Marathon wins. *Jeff Johnson photo courtesy* New England Runner.

in the men's wheelchair; and Cheri Blauwet of California, Edith Hunkeler of Switzerland, and Sherry Ramsey of Colorado in the women's wheelchair.

Other Olympians, world champions, marathon winners, and top runners have also participated in the Boston Marathon (and some were even favored) but, for one reason or another, did not live up to the pre-race press. The list is an impressive one that includes, among others, two-time Olympic Marathon champion Abebe Bikila of Ethiopia, Olympian Jim Peters of Great Britain, Olympic 10,000-meter bronze medalist Joie Ray of Illinois, Olympic Marathon gold and silver medalist Frank Shorter of Colorado, Olympic Marathon silver medalist and nine-time New York City Marathon winner Grete Waitz of Norway, and Olympic Marathon gold medalist Degaga "Mamo" Wolde of Ethiopia.

Celebrities and other notables have also run the Boston Marathon, including Lance Armstrong (2008), actress Valerie Bertinelli (2010), Super Bowl champion New England Patriot Tedy Bruschi (2012), politician Michael Dukakis (1951), actor David James Elliott (2004–05), comedic actor Will Ferrell (2003), actress Ali Landry (2002), Olympic and World Cup soccer champion Kristine Lilly (2012), television journalist Lisa Ling (2001), actor Mario Lopez (2002), and musician Joseph "Joey" McIntyre of New Kids on the Block (2013).

In less than a few hours' time on the morning of Marathon Monday, the additional tens of thousands of people fill the streets, lawns, parking lots, and fields of Hopkinton. The only official guarantee for runners to get to the start in time on race day is via the continual parade of BAA buses that commence travel at 6:00 a.m. from Copley Square in Boston to the Athletes' Village at Hopkinton High School—even when bus breakdowns occurred in 1996 for the centennial edition.

Runners, volunteers, officials, and spectators also arrive by car and bus by way of Interstate Route 495 and local roads before Hopkinton center streets close at 7:00 a.m. and the rest of the town at 7:30 a.m. The only allowed parking can be found at Hopkinton State Park (Route 85) and various South Street industrial parks and businesses. At each location, shuttle buses are provided for officials, runners, and spectators.

Accommodating the influx of marathoners is the Athletes' Village, located on the grounds of the high school and middle school complex. Located seven-tenths of a mile from the start line at the Hopkinton Town Common, this is where the BAA's Boston-based buses, as well as the track club and running club buses, drop off official entrants. The fenced-in, secured location offers plenty of portable toilets, water tables, medical stations, tent-covered areas, and open spaces. Announcements, music, and occasional stretching exercises originate in the nearby staging area.

It can be cool, cold, warm, hot, and/or wet for those pre-race hours, depending on the fickle and unpredictable New England weather of the day. In 1966, for example, for the 100th Boston Marathon, when a record 36,748 official starters descended upon the grass fields of the Athletes' Village, they were greeted with soft, wet, woodchip/hay-strewn footing. Just days prior to the momentous noontime start, snow had fallen on the region, which prompted the BAA to employ military helicopters to hover above the fields in an effort to dry the ground in time.

From about 9:10 a.m. to 10:10 a.m., the three separate fields of approximately nine thousand runners each are methodically directed to move via the adjacent Grove Street to Main Street and the corresponding corrals.

En route will be the luggage buses, where runner bags can be dropped off to be picked up at the finish. Squires advises runners what to take with them once the bags have been collected: "Remember, when you get there, have your [throwaway] rag clothes on or a bag to wear—one of those big garbage bags—if it's a wet day and for your shoes. And if it's cold, wear socks on your hands. It's like mittens, but if you also need socks later, you've got 'em. If it's hot, forget about that. If it's hot, put on an old painter's hat or something, with holes in it to breathe. And toilet paper! I'll clue ya—you'll thank me. Bring some toilet paper. You never know." Then shed said items accordingly.

And if it hasn't already sunken in, this march to the start is when the butterflies and excitement begin to build. Television helicopters chop high above for the best aerial views, the white noise of announcements and directions battle for air space alongside heart-pumping music, and the din of conversation fills whatever empty audio there is between.

The sharp and sudden warmth from being sandwiched with several thousand other bodies through the fenced-in streets can be both a blessing (in cold weather) and a curse (in hot weather). This is also where clothing can get discarded along the way, where a few last drops of water can be ingested, and where the occasional barrier-jumper can cram yet another body in the confines of the corral.

After passing through the crowd-less neighborhood roadway of Grove Street, a right-hand turn onto Route 135/Main Street and into the barricaded and roped-off corrals opens up the visual festivity and majesty of the Boston Marathon. Sidewalks and front yards are full of spectators. Race announcements can be heard a bit more clearly. And the runners wait. And wait.

The streets of the Boston Marathon are filled in the early miles. *Jeff Johnson photo courtesy* New England Runner.

While waiting, however, entrants might wonder why there is so much empty street space to their right—from the edge of the corral to the south-side curb—that is not part of the corrals. The reason, as simple as it is genius, is that the width of Main and East Main varies throughout the center of Hopkinton from about eighty-five feet in some areas and narrows to thirty-nine feet at the start line. It was decided by Dave McGillivray to set the width of the corrals to twenty-five feet in order to provide walking space outside the fencing and also to enable runners to run from a narrow part of Route 135 to a wider part at and beyond the start line. In the years prior to this realignment, it was designed conversely in that runners were packed curb to curb and were naturally forced to squeeze inward as they ran over the start line. That procedure created a massive bottleneck and a very slow and frustrating start process.

One of the streets to the right of the runners—adjacent to the Hopkinton Town Common—is Hayden Rowe Street. This was the starting point of the race between 1965 and 1985, and in 1996, it was one of the side streets used in order to accommodate the record number of entrants in the 100th Boston Marathon.

In 1966, when the men started on Hayden Rowe Street, hidden in some bushes a short distance away was Bobbi Gibb (Bingay), who, after waiting for part of the field to pass, jumped in and finished at 3:21:40, becoming the first woman to ever run the Boston Marathon (six years before the AAU and, subsequently, the BAA officially allowed women to run that distance).

The Hayden Rowe Street start was also where wheelchair division history began. In 1975, Bob Hall was promised by race director Will Cloney that if he finished the race in under three hours, he would be awarded an official certificate. With coaching leading up to the race from Squires of the Greater Boston Track Club, Hall finished in a time of 2:58:00 and became the first official wheelchair champion.

To the left of the runners, atop Main Street across from the Common, is the Korean Presbyterian Church in Greater Boston, on whose front lawn is the Douglas Duksoo Wohn–designed supine sixteen-square-foot gray marble monument in honor of the Korean athletes who have finished within the top three in the Boston Marathon. Dedicated in 2004 for the centennial of Korean immigration, three of the names are those of Boston champions: Yun Bok Suh (1947), Kee Yong Ham (1950), and Bong Joo Lee (2001).

Hours prior to the start of the race, the elite runners are bused via police escort from their Boston accommodations to the former First Congregational Church, just yards from the Hopkinton start line. In the secured environs of the church basement, they spend their pre-race time relaxing, preparing, and/or fidgeting. Accompanied by their agents and coaches, the top athletes mingle amongst themselves and follow their own routines, which can include stretching, communing, pacing, and conversing. Some lay down with their legs up on the wall, some plug in their headphones and focus, and others might visualize the race or talk to people to pass the time. Food, fluids, mats, and other amenities are provided, and there are numerous volunteers to attend to any request the competitors might have. This area is one of the few where the runners can collect themselves in relative privacy outside the view of fans and the media.

Closer to their start time, the runners begin to venture outdoors to the rear parking lot, which is partially hidden from view but still often surrounded by spectators and onlookers leaning against the police barricades. After some close-quarter strides and stretches, they are then called in seeded and gender order to align with the succession of the various starts—top ten women, next subsequent seeded women, masters, etc. Shortly before the start gun, the assembled formation walks single file through a six-foot-wide corral from the parking lot to the open space of East Main Street and the start line, where last-minute strides and warm-ups occur. This is repeated for the men in time for their respective separate starts shortly thereafter.

Located next door, to the east, is the Main Street Cemetery. For years, it was through this graveyard that the elite men and women would walk on their way to the start line. The juxtaposition of the fittest athletes in the world passing by those who have passed was not lost on observers. The elite athletes now walk to the start around the southwest perimeter.

To the right of the runners is Hopkinton Town Common, which is filled with a long, welcomed row of portable toilets. Booths selling souvenirs, clothing, and such forbidden pre-race treats as Italian sausage, fried dough, burgers, and hot dogs also fill the area. The Common is also home to several nods of reverence to the Boston Marathon, including the bisection of paths called Johnny Kelley Crossing, named after the two-time winner (1935, 1945) who started a record sixty-one Bostons and finished a record fifty-eight; Marathon Way, the access road that parallels East Main Street; and *The Starter*, the eighty-inch-tall Michael Alfano statue of BAA athletic director George V. Brown, who was the official race starter from 1905 to 1937. Except for in 1990 (BAA president Joann Flaminio), the race since 1905 has been started by a Brown family member, including former BAA president Walter A. Brown from 1938 to 1942, George V. Brown Jr. from 1943 to 1968 and 1970 to 1980, Paul V. Brown in 1969, former BAA president Thomas J. Brown from 1981 to 1989, and former BAA board of governor member Walter F. Brown since 1991.

At various points on Route 135, between the current start line that began in 1986 and the downhill portion toward the Ashland town line, is where the Boston Marathon started from 1957 to 1964 (a short distance beyond the current start), 1927 to 1956 (farther east), and 1924 to 1926 (still farther east).

For twenty-one years, from 1965 to 1985, the start of the Boston Marathon was located on Hayden Rowe Street, shown here between the house in the middle and starter Paul V. Brown (center). Crowd control was at a minimum as spectators hung from trees and closed in on race officials. *Courtesy Tom Burke.*

Walter A. Brown, who founded the Boston Celtics of the National Basketball Association and was also president of the Boston Athletic Association from 1941 to 1964, was the official race starter for five years (1938–42). *Courtesy Tom Burke.*

Located on the Center School grounds near Hopkinton Town Common is the *Yes You Can* statue of Team Hoyt, the inspirational multiple-sport duo of Dick Hoyt and his son Rick Hoyt, a spastic quadriplegic who lives with cerebral palsy. *Photo by Paul C. Clerici.*

Facing the northeast side of the Common is the Mike Tabor–created bronze *Yes You Can* statue on the front lawn of the Center School on Ash Street. It depicts the father-son duo of Dick Hoyt and Rick Hoyt, known collectively as Team Hoyt. Rick, a spastic quadriplegic who was born with cerebral palsy, sits in a specially designed wheelchair that his father, Dick, pushes—a feat accomplished in over 1,100 events, including a half dozen Ironman triathlons and thirty Boston Marathons. This location is also the starting point for the elite wheelchair athletes, who line up in a grid formation and are then escorted via Ash Street to the start line.

Near the start line, formed by Route 135 to the north, Marathon Way to the south, and Ash Street and the BAA's registration office to the east, is a triangular median of grass called Cookie's Corner, so named in honor of Colonel Richard "Cookie" Kumlin, who for years had taken care of this and other veteran-related landscapes. Situated in the middle is a monument to the local veterans of World War I, a larger-than-life statue and granite base that reaches high above for an unobstructed bird's-eye view of the start. Affectionately known as the Doughboy Statue, it depicts a soldier walking toward the direction of the oncoming runners. A plaque on it reads, "To honor the men of Hopkinton who served in the World War 1917–1919." On Patriots' Day Monday, this special swath of land is the centerpiece of the large barricaded and secured media/VIP/dignitary staging area from which the races are started.

Located to the right of the wide and colorful start line is the large staging area. Several notable people—a Brown family member, former Boston champions, politicians, local celebrity athletes, etc.—fire the electronic gun from the stage to start the various races. Excitement builds with each start as the slow, semi-walking pace takes runners by the stage and off to Boston.

Leading up to that gun, one of the first things a runner should do, according to Squires, is find a position in the corral. "Yes. Position is the most important thing," he affirms. "When you get to the start, please go to the far left of the course. Hang out there. Don't stay on the right side because they'll push you into the middle, and you're going to get kicked and shoved [to] where you don't want to be. There's always people on the edge that drag you in. As I always say, the sheep go right, and you're going to stay left. And eventually, at about two miles for some people, you can move your way near the middle."

The 165-foot drop over about the first three-quarters of a mile at the onset is immediate and potentially dangerous. A case in point was the 1987 Boston Marathon, when several wheelchair athletes collided right after the start—mostly due to the slick, recently paved course and an uncontrolled descent. (Now, before they can begin to race on their own, wheelchair athletes have a controlled downhill start for the first quarter of a mile; it was a half-mile when first instituted, and it returns to that distance if it is raining.) Runners in 1987 also fared poorly at the start when a lack of coordinated communications resulted in some of the frontrunners tripping over the rope that race volunteers used to stretch across the line to prevent false starts (Dave McGillivray replaced the rope with a human chain of volunteers).

But all athletes should be prepared. Squires cautions, "You've done enough training so that you know the course. You know what that downhill is like. But it's possible that you're going to be bumping around. This isn't the usual marathon you're going to be in. I don't care what group you're in, you're going to run faster than you want to because of the downhill throwing you."

Squires points out that the start is so dense and quick that even when the occasional entrant trips, the collective mass of the constantly moving force can keep them upright and proceeding forward. "I've seen it! They fell, but guess what? They were held up because [the field] was so thick! The first 150 yards is a brute. It's very sharp. Extremely!"

Runners stay on Route 135 for the first half of the race. In Hopkinton, that means East Main Street for just under two miles and then onto West Union Street.

For runners who desire fluids at each mile, there is no water station at the first or last mile markers. Twenty-four staggered stations—located first on the right-hand side and then immediately on the left to reduce potential bottlenecks and collisions—are located from the second mile to the twenty-fifth.

"This is what to do," said Squires. "Take a bottle of water with you, and when you get to a mile [marker], drink. Do this for the first four or five miles [until the field begins to thin]. Stay in the middle of the road after a while. This way, you won't get caught going to get water, and you're safe in the middle. After it starts to spread out, throw the bottle away." This is important because there have been hard collisions, broken bones, and angry tempers in the chaos.

What can be found at the first mile marker, on the left of the runners, is *The Spirit of the Marathon* statue, located at the Weston Nurseries Garden Center. Facing the runners, the fourteen-foot, 3,400-pound Mico Kaufman–designed monument shows 1946 Boston Marathon champion Stylianos Kyriakides sprinting skyward alongside the "spirit" of fellow Greek marathoner Spyridon Louis, who won the 1896 Modern Olympic Marathon in Athens, Greece. Thanks in large part to Dimitri Kyriakides, the son of the late Boston winner; local New Balance Athletic Shoes; and the 26.2 Foundation, this statue in 2006 (as well as an identical one in the town of Marathon, Greece, in 2004) came to fruition.

Squires smiles and says, "When you go by, on your left side—the side you're still running on—you can give him a tip of your hat. It's still congested, and you're probably still running a lot faster than you want to because the crowds are pushing you through. But don't move out to the middle of the course yet because when it turns, it bunches up again."

At this point, still within the first mile or so, the field is jammed, the roadway is crooked, and runners are constantly exiting and entering from the sides to unofficially join the run, tie shoes, stretch out, high-five supporters, relieve themselves, etc. And speaking of relief in these early mile wooded areas, whereas the men can make use of the plentiful trees, the recent addition of rows of hay bales have provided equal discretion for the women.

And as far as running in and out of people on the course to find the perfect spot, "Don't jockey around," Squires warns. "It's a waste of energy. And there could be a group behind you who are over-racing and are going to run like heck and find you."

Hopkinton covers the first 1.90 miles. Ashland is next.

CHAPTER 3

ASHLAND:
MILES 1.90 TO 4.95

I t all started here in 1897." That's what an old sign once posted on the Pleasant Street site of the ol' Metcalf's Mill announced with pride. And it is also true, of course.

Early reports indicate that the current land of Ashland was first named by the Natick Indians as the Village of Magunkaquog in the mid-seventeenth century and, in the early 1800s, was called Unionville as part of the towns of Framingham, Holliston, and Hopkinton. By 1837, however, the small town of 130 sought its independence. After several years of petitions and court rulings, it finally separated itself and in 1846 was incorporated as Ashland, named for the myriad ash trees on the land—in Kentucky! The town name was chosen by a leading resident, James Jackson, based on his admiration of the "Great Compromiser" Henry Clay, a state representative, U.S. senator, Speaker of the House, secretary of state, and presidential candidate from Kentucky who so named his plantation estate in Lexington.

In 1916, Henry E. Warren invented what would become the electronic clock when he developed "synchronizing timers," and because of this, Ashland is also known as the "Clock Town."

When BAA officials on bicycles decided to embark on the marathon distance from the oval track on Irvington Street in Boston, they eventually followed the accessibility of travel via the Boston and Albany Railroad line, which stopped in Ashland and could transport runners, spectators, supporters, and officials.

There were eighteen entrants for that first run. And when U.S. Olympic double-gold medalist Thomas Burke of the BAA marked the start line with his heel across the dirt road of Pleasant Street near Alvah Metcalf's packing-box mill on Patriots' Day Monday, April 19, 1897, fifteen men toed that line. At Burke's direct and simple command of "Go!" just shy of twenty minutes past noon, history began running.

The athletes were followed throughout the race by every imaginable means of transport: bicycles, motorcycles, wagons, carriages, and the occasional watering cart and electric car. Of the ten runners who finished the race (24.5 miles, according to the BAA; 25 miles reported in the *Boston Globe* newspaper), the winner in 2:55:10 was John J. McDermott, who would also come in fourth place the following year, when a Boston College student from Canada, Ronald J. MacDonald, cut more than thirteen minutes off that time to win in 2:42:00. The number of starters (twenty-one) and finishers (fifteen) also grew that second year.

The 1897 and 1898 races were the only ones to start from Pleasant. When it was decided to finish the race at the BAA clubhouse on Exeter Street in Boston, the start subsequently moved westward (or behind the first start) three-tenths of a mile to the Boston and Albany Railroad Bridge. It was on that High Street bridge that the next eight races (1899–1906) would start, and it was also where the only false start and restart in Boston Marathon history would occur.

An increase in interest put a strain on the start logistics, as the width of the bridge was only so wide and could accommodate only so many. The ninth Marathon, in 1905, fielded a record eighty-four men on the bridge, and 1906 expanded to eighty-six. It was determined to once again move the start, which the BAA did in 1907 to the Valentine farmland on Hopkinton Road at Steven's Corner in Ashland. The start remained there for the next seventeen years (1907–23) before it moved farther westward to the neighboring town of Hopkinton for the 1924 running.

In 1910, Fred Cameron of Canada led from the first mile to win the fourteenth Marathon, besting Clarence DeMar, who came in second place.

For generations, the only physical acknowledgment marking the historical reference point in Ashland was a small white stone slab with "B 25" engraved in black at the commuter rail tracks, mostly hidden several dozen yards from the original site (where it still remains).

At the turn of the twenty-first century, interest to clean up the mill site adjacent to the Sudbury River Reservoir resulted in a multi-year project that began with a simple sign of declaration (similar in design to the one

One of the celebratory plaques at Marathon Park in Ashland—the site of the original start of the Boston Marathon—features information on all twenty-seven races that began in Ashland, which includes nine course records, twenty-three different winers, one four-time champion (Clarence DeMar), one two-time winner (John Caffery) and the Camp Devens Divisional Team victors of the 1918 relay. *Courtesy Ashland Sporting Association.*

Left: At the Steven's Corner start line in 1912, the final start-line location in Ashland, Boston Marathon runners prepare for the sixteenth annual event. *Courtesy The Sports Museum of New England/Ashland Historical Society*.

Opposite: This stone marker in Ashland is located near the railroad tracks and the Pleasant Street site of the first two Boston Marathon races, which were held approximately twenty-five miles west of Boston. *Photo by Paul C. Clerici*.

annually displayed at Hopkinton Town Common that featured the outline of the Bay State and a silhouetted runner) nailed to one of the sturdy mill-site trees.

Years later, to fully commemorate the first twenty-seven editions of the Boston Marathon in the town of Ashland, the revered site of Metcalf's Mill, the remnants of which can still be seen even after a fire destroyed it in the 1930s, was christened as Marathon Park. It is located about a half mile from the center of Ashland and on the opposite side of the Massachusetts Bay Transportation Authority (MBTA) rapid transit Ashland commuter rail station from the West Union Street entrance off the Boston Marathon course.

In 2003, a granite monument was dedicated to the "Keepers of the Flame: 1928–1983"—Bob Campbell, referee, champion runner; Scottie McFetridge, chief track official; Jerry Nason, sports writer [*sic*]; Tony Nota, chief timer; Jock Semple, RPT (registered physical therapist), runner,

MARATHON PARK *IT ALL S*

Clarence DeMar: The Immortal

Clarence Harrison DeMar was a newspaper printer who lived in the Highlands section of Melrose, Massachusetts.

He worked on Boston's Newspaper Row, a hotbed of journalistic combat since colonial days. At the dawn of the 20th century eight newspapers — the Record, Herald, Advertiser, Globe, American, Post, Journal and Traveler — published daily near Post Office Square.

For decades, day in and day out, DeMar stood ready at the printers' union "shape-up". Once declared fit for work and assigned to a paper, he labored hard under harsh conditions in one of these human pressure cookers.

The "comp room" of every paper in the neighborhood was essentially the same, one or another variety of hell on earth.

Hundreds of printers and editors, their stubborn yet urgent chatter altogether deafening, wedged themselves into these poorly lit basement chambers wide abeam yet cursed with low-slung ceilings. Every shift these dank, dusty cellars filled with tobacco smoke and sour whiffs of liquor recently consumed.

Buildings rattled as nearby presses constantly rolled off papers, their labors humming a dull relentless tune. Editors approved hand-set racks of type then stepped aside as printers wielding hand-held sledgehammers slammed frames of tiny metal type characters into intricate metal page forms tilted onto huge slate tablets.

Hot, smoky, poisonous fumes steamed from ever-present molten lead pots, the malleable metal within dangerous, deadly and soon to slither into the nooks and crannies of the page form, locking it in, the key to success. The press bells rang and rang, and the deadline, always another deadline, bore down like a locomotive, the next edition more important than the last.

This trade, lost to a digital age, was never a labor of love. Working "hot metal" at a daily newspaper was no joke, requiring not only the ability to perform quickly and accurately under tremendous stress and adverse conditions but also the biblical patience of Job, the strength and stamina of a circus strongman and the attention to minute details that any watchmaker would be proud to possess. Tough work, rough tools, diverse skills, unique men.

His efforts in those infernal rooms were how DeMar at first supported his mother and five younger siblings and then later his wife and his five children. But everybody needs a diversion, something to bring life into balance.

Some colleagues gambled, but many just crawled into a bottle. Not DeMar. No. In his spare time, he became an immortal.

Before the '20s roared, before Babe Ruth hit it big, Knute Rockne assembled "The Four Horsemen" or Jack Dempsey ruled the "Sweet Science, there was Clarence DeMar. Call him "Mr. DeMarathon". Everybody did.

He didn't run for the prize money. There was none. He didn't run for the fame. A religious man, a lay preacher, he considered the spotlight's glare a devil's playground.

Instead DeMar ran for the sport's simplicity, pursuing perfection through preparation. But he loved to race for the sense of self-worth it provided, of being the best at something. As a young man, DeMar took to the roads, chasing excellence, and that motivation propelled him up to the apex of distance running's pyramid.

DeMar remains there a century later but time marches on, obscuring his accomplishments.

First sporting North Dorchester AA and later Melrose Legion Post colors, DeMar ran 33 "Bostons", winning seven: 1911,1922,1923,1924, 1927,1928 and 1930, the first three starting right here in Ashland. He owns the permanent course record at the 40K Ashland distance, set in 1922 with a time of 2 hours, 18 minutes, 10 seconds.

He won his first "Boston" at age 22 and his last at 41. A total unknown, he burst upon the Ashland scene in 1910, finishing second, and 11 times he finished in the top 3 and 15 times in top 10. He finished seventh in 1938 at age 49 and ran his last "Boston" in 1954 at age 65, finishing 78th in an open field of 113 starters.

Only three other men have won "Boston" as many as four times (as of 2012): French Canadian Gerard Cote in the 1940s; "Boston Billy" Rodgers in the late 1970s and 1980; and Kenyan Robert Kipkoech Cheruiyot inside the years 2003-08.

Winning in three different decades, DeMar captured seven laurel wreaths and, amazingly, after those seven victories he reportedly worked as usual those evenings and oftentimes set the front-page headlin reporting his own victory to Boston rea

Showing Spartan grit those ancient C would admire, legend has it DeMar wo back and forth from work each day, su sleet or snow, a distance of about eig each way. Donning a fresh shirt, he wo standing up for a full shift then run bac

DeMar competed for 49 years, until the 69, in over 1,000 races, including ove 25 miles or more. On St. Patrick's Day he won a 44-mile race from Providence to in 5:41:37. His last race, a 15K in Bath, 1957, he finished 14th, a year before his

DeMar died of cancer in Reading four d turning 70 on June 11, 1958. A few days he crawled outside and worked in his g his widow said, adding, "He just would

As part of the revitalization of the original start-line area of the Boston Marathon in Ashland, the site has been named Marathon Park and several informational plaques have been installed, including this one that celebrates Clarence DeMar's remarkable seven victories, three of which started in Ashland. *Courtesy Ashland Sporting Association.*

trainer—whose dogged perseverance and reverence of the race continued its legacy and history.

In 2012, the old and forgotten sign—"Welcome to Ashland: It all started here in 1897: Ashland to Boston 25 miles"—that had been nailed to a tree

TED HERE

In his own way he was every bit as much a giant as Ruth, Grange, Tilden, Sandy or any of the legendary figures of The Roaring '20s. And yet, he was largely unknown — for the Boston Marathon had not caught on in America as yet.

— HALL OF FAME SPORTSWRITER JOE FALLS,
Comparing Clarence DeMar to the titans of baseball, football, tennis and horse racing of the early 20th Century in his 1977 book, "The Boston Marathon: The incredible zany story of America's greatest foot race...".

nce DeMar,
bound for
rd in 1922.

erceived heart problem held him back
uring the peak years of his 20s. He won
in" in 1911 against the advice of his
who told him he had a heart murmur.
pped "Boston" until 1917. Restless, he
ed to Ashland and, out of form, finished
again rebelling against doctor's advice.
as soon drafted into the Army for World
and underwent a stringent military
al, its findings discounting any heart
ms. His military service prevented him
unning "Boston" again until 1922.
e 65, he underwent rigorous tests and
art was found to be unusually healthy. Like
er Boston sports icon, Ted Williams, one

must wonder what records DeMar would hold if he had run in those eight prime years, five lost due to his doctor, three as an Army private.

When DeMar first won "Boston" in 1911 he was 5-foot-8 tall and weighed 127 pounds. After years of training, when he won his last, 19 years later in 1930, he surprisingly had gained 15 pounds, tipping the scales at 142.

In the "Roaring 20s" when a dinner of Beef Wellington chased by a few Brandy Alexanders and finished with a fat stogie was thought healthy, DeMar again chose his own path. An early believer that diet and rest could extend athletic prowess, he watched what he ate: plenty of fruits and vegetables washed down with lots of milk; and he slept 8-9 hours a night.

Always self-reliant, DeMar invariably believed in himself. He didn't like or trust coaching. He served as his own tutor, his own motivator, writing in his autobiography that "when I run, I am in supreme command of my destiny."

He chaffed under the reins placed upon him in three Olympics (1912, '24 & '28). His heart set on gold, he medaled only once, a bronze in 1924 at Paris, and placed the blame for those failures squarely on those coaches. DeMar's was the last American marathon medal until Frank Shorter's gold 48 years later in Munich.

Born into poverty on June 7, 1888 in Madeira, Ohio, he was the oldest of six children whose father was dead by the time he was 10. DeMar helped support his family by running to nearby hamlets and peddling trinkets, sometimes earning as much as 50 cents a day.

The struggling family then moved to tiny Warwick in north-central Massachusetts. Shortly thereafter, his overwhelmed mother placed DeMar at the Farm and Trade School on Thompson's Island in Boston Harbor, where he took up cross country and graduated as class valedictorian.

He then went to work on a Vermont farm and, for several years, put himself through the University of Vermont. He left in his junior year to rejoin his mother, this time in Melrose, and found the printer's job needed to again help support his family. He also took up the sport of road racing with purpose.

Determined to succeed, he dismissed critics of his alleged awkward running style writing that, in essence, distance running is "the ability to get there as quickly as possible" and to "run like hell and get the agony over with."

Said to be hard of hearing, DeMar had a taciturn manner and made few friends among his fellow runners. He was often annoyed by the antics of spectators and several times reportedly slugged fans who crossed his path during a race and once allegedly kicked a dog.

DeMar married wife Margaret at 40 and they began their family of five children. Basically shy and thus stingy in public with the spoken word, he nonetheless became a Sunday School teacher and a Boy Scout Troop leader.

He worked with his hands but was also a man of letters, attending Boston University and Harvard and attaining an Associates' degree in printing science. He owned his own print shop and taught printing and coached track at Keene Normal School, now Keene State College, while living in New Hampshire in the 1930s.

For a man who spoke sparingly, he was a prolific writer, composing many magazine articles on distance running. In 1936, DeMar penned his autobiography. As lean as his lifestyle, this extraordinary man summed up his amazing accomplishments in just 92 pages.

When one hears about running in the footsteps of legends here in Ashland, one need not look further than Clarence DeMar, a runner without parallel, a competitor without peer.

A true immortal.

was replaced by a beautifully designed cobalt-blue freestanding Marathon Park sign by Lou Mancini, complete with reliefs of several runners in the middle and the proclamation "Ashland 1897: It all started here." In a ceremony with town, state, and BAA officials, it was unveiled in front of cheerful spectators eighteen days prior to the 116th Boston Marathon.

In October 2013, during the weekend of the second annual Ashland Half Marathon & 5K road races, six informative display plaques were unveiled throughout the park. On hand to perform the honors were Bill Rodgers;

Just after runners enter Ashland is TJ's Fine Food & Spirits (left), from which patrons continuously yell and cheer for marathoners throughout the race. *Photo by Paul C. Clerici.*

Shortly after four miles is a traffic island of which runners need to be aware, although the race distance is reportedly the same on both sides. *Photo by Paul C. Clerici.*

Bobbi Gibb; BAA executive director Tom Grilk; Patrick Kennedy, the great-grandnephew of 1917 champion William "Bill" Kennedy; and Jean Cunis of Ashland, who was born the year the 1918 Boston Marathon held a military team relay due to World War I.

Back on the course, immediately to the left of the runners upon entering Ashland on West Union Street is TJ's Fine Food & Spirits, an always joyful and boisterous eatery of spectators who seem to cheer for every single marathoner who passes by the friendly pub, which also offers a special Marathon Day Breakfast Buffet. Whether from the music being played or the roars of the patrons, the early support is nonstop. Also heard on the streets of Ashland, thanks to a neighbor's speaker system, is a continuous loop of Bill Conti's "Gonna Fly Now" theme song from *Rocky*.

The first official water station is at the two-mile mark, and this is also where it can get tricky. Beware of runners who dart to the side seemingly out of nowhere, for many a collision can occur at these early stations.

"Stay good," said Squires, who would always bring his athletes—including Boston's "Duel in the Sun" runner-up Dick Beardsley of Minnesota and Boston Marathon winners Bill Rodgers, Alberto Salazar of Massachusetts, and Greg Meyer of Massachusetts—to Ashland High School to begin their intense champion-caliber training on the course. "You're still dropping [in elevation]. And there's a [traffic] island and the road twists and turns. And when you get to four miles, it gets narrower then. Run smart."

On a gentle downhill at the 4K (2.49 miles) mark is where the last of the Ashland start lines was located. In this area—just before the Ashland Community Center and the Ashland State Park to the right of the runners—is where the Boston Marathon started for seventeen years (1907–23) near West Union and Frankland Streets. West Union Street becomes East Union Street at 3.00 miles and then Union Street at 6K (3.72 miles).

Of note around the four-mile area is where, in 1967, Kathrine Virginia Switzer entered, or more precisely, was pushed into, history. At the time, the AAU did not officially allow women to compete in the marathon distance and, as a result, the Boston Marathon. When the twenty-year-old from Syracuse University registered as K.V. Switzer—admittedly something she did in a nod to some of her literary heroes who did likewise with their names—she received a bib number and joined the field on Patriots' Day. Upon seeing a woman running with a bib number, larger-than-life race official Semple, with great animation and frenetic action, leapt off the media vehicle and unsuccessfully tried to remove the number and Switzer to no avail—and right in front of the press truck. Pictures of the altercation made their way to the newspapers, and as they say, the rest is (more) history.

Route 135 continues after Union Street to Waverly Street from 7K (4.34 miles) in Ashland to 12K (7.45 miles) in Framingham.

Ashland contains 3.05 miles of the course, and runners exit the town just prior to the fifth mile for Framingham.

CHAPTER 4

FRAMINGHAM:

MILES 4.95 TO 7.52

About a decade after the *Mayflower* brought the Pilgrims to settle in Plymouth, the Massachusetts Bay Colony in 1630 received aid from the Connecticut Indians, who would travel along what would become known as the Old Connecticut Path. Massachusetts Bay Colony deputy governor Thomas Danforth, who in the late 1690s would serve as a judge in the witch trials in Salem, Massachusetts, over the years expanded his real estate to some fifteen thousand acres that he named Framlingham. Spelled with the letter "l" in the middle, he named it after his hometown in England, which dates back centuries.

With such an expanse of land, Danforth was the greatest opponent to the wishes of those who wanted a town. It wasn't until after he died, in late 1699, that those wishes were fulfilled when, exactly seven months later, on June 5, 1700, the town of Framingham was incorporated.

Interestingly (and in regard to the Boston Marathon's connection to Patriots' Day and the Battles of Lexington and Concord), two months before the "shot heard 'round the world" (wrote Ralph Waldo Emerson) at the North Bridge in Concord that began the Revolutionary War in 1775, British general Thomas Gage had dispatched troops to map out a route to Worcester for his British invasion. Having spotted Minutemen in military exercises in Framingham, Gage rerouted his battle plan to the border towns of Lexington and Concord.

On the course, runners are greeted with the 8K mark (4.98 miles) immediately before the town line and the 5.00-mile mark right after. This is also where the course begins to level and widen for some much-needed breathing room.

On the wide streets of Framingham in 1975, top runners include (from left) 1970 winner Ron Hill of Great Britain (1), two-time runner-up Tom Fleming (2), Richard Mabuza of Swaziland (63), 1977 winner Jerome Drayton of Canada (5), and four-time winner Bill Rodgers (14). *Jeff Johnson photo courtesy* New England Runner.

"The minute you hit the Framingham town line, you won't encounter any road as narrow as you came over from Hopkinton to now," Squires pointed out. "It's starting to open out a little bit wider, and after the next mile, you're into the widest road of the whole course."

A sharp left-hand turn takes runners to mile six and then, two-tenths of a mile later, the 10K, between which the Melchiorri Dixieland Hobos of Natick at one time played on the rooftop of a car dealership. It would always put a smile on a runner's face, especially when the chords of "When the Saints Go Marching In" broke them out of a daze and they'd look around to see from where the music was originating.

"That was when you come off a very narrow road," said Squires, "and finally get to something like a boulevard. Lots of room."

After running through close neighborhoods, this part of Route 135 on Waverly Street presents a wide vista and screaming spectators (overhead horizontal railroad crossing lights even seem to frame the view).

To the left of the runners can be seen—and heard, when the horn blows—the commuter rail train on the Framingham/Worcester line. At

When marathoners enter Framingham, they immediately cross the 8K marker at right and, shortly thereafter, the five-mile marker, also at right. *Photo by Paul C. Clerici.*

U.S. Army National Guard members (right) watch over the runners and spectators at the seven-mile mark in Framingham. *Photo by Paul C. Clerici.*

It was near this Framingham commuter rail train station where, during the 1907 Boston Marathon, a freight train cut off the field of runners from the lead pack. *Photo by Paul C. Clerici.*

around the seven-mile mark is the landmark expansive-roofed, stone-built Framingham train station, with its familiar green-and-white window awnings to the runners' left, and railroad tracks in front that cut across the roadway.

During the 1907 Boston Marathon, eventual winner Thomas Longboat, a Canadian Onandaga Indian, and 5 other top runners battled not only rain and sleet but also an incoming freight train! After they were able to cross the tracks and continue toward Boston, the train proceeded onward—across the street—and forced the remaining field of nearly 120 men to wait behind them for over a minute. When it was all over, only Thomas Longboat in first and future Olympic Marathon gold medalist John "Johnny" Hayes of New York in third prevented a Massachusetts sweep, as the men in second, fourth, and fifth places were from the Bay State.

A party atmosphere swells along this portion, as several block parties, closed-off parking-lot parties, and pub and restaurant gatherings cheer on the marathoners as they head toward Natick.

But before the runners cross the town line at about 7.5 miles, on their right is Hansen Electrical Supply Inc., a nondescript gray building that nearly every marathoner looks to during his or her run. Why? Because of the sixteen large, adjacent vertical panes of glass, whose reflective nature

To the constant cheers throughout the course, the inspirational Team Hoyt duo of Dick Hoyt and his son Rick pass through Framingham at the site of the landmark train station. *Bill Boyle photo courtesy* New England Runner.

serves as an enormous mirror where runners can spot-check their posture. This fact is also announced on a sign that marathoners can read as they approach the business. Even the sidewalk area in front is cordoned off to allow unobstructed viewing.

Throughout the Boston Marathon, spectators often keep runners updated on the score of the morning's Red Sox game. *Photo by Paul C. Clerici.*

And before leaving Framingham, on sidewalks and streets, there are the first of many makeshift signs that begin to appear with updates of the Boston Red Sox game. With but a few exceptions, since 1959 there has been a baseball game at Fenway Park on the day of the race. And since 1968, there has been a morning first pitch so that the end of the game can coincide with the elite marathoners passing through nearby Kenmore Square (although with the earlier race start time, the leaders pass by Fenway Park while the game is still on).

There is also a Framingham–Red Sox connection in that there are no fewer than three BoSox players with ties to this town in pitcher Roger Clemens, catcher Rich Gedman, and infielder Lou Merloni. (There's also former Houston Astros general manager Talbot "Tal" Smith, fourteen-year/seven-team player Mark Sweeney, and Pittsburgh Pirates 1948 National Baseball Hall of Fame inductee Harold "Pie" Traynor.) As for Natick, right next door, you can add former player and Red Sox batting coach Walt Hriniak to the roster.

Runners are in Framingham for 2.57 miles before entering Natick.

CHAPTER 5

NATICK:

MILES 7.52 TO 11.72

Just after 7.5 miles, runners enter the "place of hills." An ominous name for any stretch of a marathon course, this is how the town of Natick is known in the native language of the local "Praying Indians." John Eliot, a Puritan minister, established the town in 1651 and was also instrumental in teaching and preaching in both English and the native language of the Praying Indians, as there were several similar "Praying Indian towns" in the area.

Any peaceful and harmonious existence slowly died in the late 1600s when King Philip—also known as Metacomet, son of Chief Massasoit—forged an attack on the white population. Out of fear and ignorance, a court order was then passed to ostracize the Indians to Deer Island in Boston Harbor some twenty-five miles due east. Between the harsh island conditions and nothing of theirs to which they returned, they eventually disappeared.

Route 135 becomes West Central Street in Natick at 8.0 miles. At about 8.5 miles on Marathon Monday often stands a jolly fellow in a red suit with white gloves and a beard as white as snow. Even in the extreme heat of some of the hottest Boston Marathon races can be seen ol' Saint Nick waving from a sidewalk to the runners' right. The strange (and early) juxtaposition always seems to elicit smiles from the tired runners, who at the very least instantly think of cooler temperatures when it's hot.

About eight miles into the 1909 Boston Marathon (a bit off from the current eight-mile mark due to the different start-line location back then in Ashland), Howard Pearce, in one of the hottest races on record, stepped off the course and into a vehicle to be taken to Boston. No problem there.

Eight months before Christmas, even ol' Saint Nick can put a smile on runners' faces as they pass by in Natick. *Photo by Paul C. Clerici.*

However, upon entering the city, he stepped back onto the course and nearly crossed the finish line. Problem. But eventual winner Henri Renaud of New Hampshire was not denied the exclusivity of the victory, as the obstinate Howard Pearce was pulled off the course in time. A similar incident occurred at the 1916 Boston Marathon when E.F. Merchant reportedly rode in a car for a portion of the race after suffering leg cramps but then returned to the race some miles later. He was disqualified.

A half mile later, at nine miles, runners pass by Fiske Pond and the waters of Lake Cochituate. The occasional fisherman can be seen on a canoe and a few others casting their lines from the edge of the road, all seemingly oblivious to the masses pounding their way to Boston. Here, the course is wide and it is flat.

"It's wide enough that you're not going to be cramped in," said Squires. "You have about six miles of good roads."

This is also a point of great legend in Boston Marathon history. "Yeah, this is it," said Squires in reference to whether or not Ellison "Tarzan" Brown, a two-time Boston winner and Narragansett Indian, dove in for an impromptu swim during one of his Boston Marathon runs. "But he didn't swim. He kicked off his shoes, walked to the water, sat on a rock [because the water was closer to the embankment], shook his feet in the water and then put his

Above: At the 1981 Boston Marathon, when Toshihiko Seko of Japan (right) won and Craig Virgin came in second, spectators still crowded the streets—on the streets—and police motorcycles still rode close to the lead runners. *Photo by Leo Kulinski Jr.*

Left: In the 1979 Boston Marathon, Tom Fleming (left) finished fourth and Bob Hodge third. Both American runners routinely ran in the top ten at Boston, as Fleming also came in second (1973, 1974), third (1975), sixth (1977) and tenth (1978), and Hodge was also sixth (1986). *Photo by Leo Kulinski Jr.*

The center of Natick is full of spectators, music, and support of all kinds to which the marathoners look forward. *Photo by Paul C. Clerici.*

shoes back on. I think the paper said something like 'cools his tootsies off.'"
Legend or not, Fiske or Cochituate, 'tis Boston!

At the ten-mile mark, runners can begin to see—peering from above the trees—the steeple of the First Congregational Church of Natick, a great point of reference for the heart of the town. Just before the center of town, to the left of the runners, are exuberant spectators and singers serenading the people. The American Legion Natick Post 107 also drapes a huge American flag on its building, the sharp flapping sound of which can be heard on windy days.

And on hot race days, the Natick Fire Department, also on the left, sets up cooling stations and fire-hose sprays on its driveway to cool off the marathoners. This, plus the cheers from the massive crowds of people on the Natick Town Common to the right of the runners, lifts the spirits of the tired.

"Don't push it," Squires warned about feeling good at this point. "You should! You should feel good. Stay cool."

About a half mile away is a celebratory group of neighbors who, every year on their front lawn, construct some kind of edifice that is both attractive and useful. In the past, it has included a two-story replica of the cable-stayed Leonard P. Zakim Bunker Hill Memorial Bridge in Boston, the left-field

Above: When it's a hot Boston Marathon, the Natick Fire Department provides cooling stations of water sprays and tents on its driveway in the center of town. *Photo by Paul C. Clerici.*

Left: Bill Rodgers, shown here winning the 1980 Boston Marathon, did not finish his first Boston attempt in 1973; stopped a few times when he won in 1975; set American records when he won in 1975 and 1979; and is a four-time winner of the Boston Marathon and New York City Marathon. *Photo by Leo Kulinski Jr.*

Green Monster of Fenway Park, and even a facsimile of a two-story house sans an exterior wall. On each, the people sit, eat, cheer, and make merry!

This area is also where West Central Street changes to East Central Street at 17K (10.56 miles). The last portion of Natick continues to feature good-sized flat neighborhood miles, but that soon changes when runners enter the next town at just under 12.00 miles.

Natick covers 4.20 miles. Next up is Wellesley.

CHAPTER 6

WELLESLEY:

MILES 11.72 TO 15.93

At just under 12.00 miles (11.72, to be precise), runners enter Contentment—perhaps not with their own physical state (or maybe so) but rather in this former town whose name it was in the mid-1600s. This land was first purchased from the local Indians and prospered as part of what was called Dedham, which was incorporated in 1636, a mere six years after Boston was named. In 1711, Dedham spawned the town of Needham, as well a smaller section called West Needham.

In West Needham lived the Welles family, including Isabella Pratt Welles, who, while in France in 1835, was courted by and married Horatio Hollis Hunnewell, a Watertown, Massachusetts native who was working overseas in the Welles & Co. banking business. Upon their return home, the Welles family continued to devote themselves to West Needham, and as a result of their benevolence, the town voted to change the name of its post office to Wellesley in 1862.

Shortly thereafter, in 1870, Hunnewell's neighbors Henry and Pauline Durant founded the Wellesley Female Seminary, which later became Wellesley College in 1873. Eight years hence, in 1881 with the able assistance of Hunnewell and Durant, among others, the town of Wellesley was born.

Upon entering the town of Wellesley, to the right of the runners can be seen the beautiful five-hundred-acre campus of Wellesley College—the third of the so-called Seven Sisters colleges that composed the original group of women's liberal arts colleges in the Northeast region of the United States. Within about a mile, runners can hear the low din of what's become known

Left: In the years prior to stringent qualifying standards, Boston Marathon fields were still manageable, such as when Greater Boston Track Club teammates Don Ricciato (3011) and Jack McDonald (2716) ran in 1977, when there were 3,040 official entrants and 2,329 official finishers. *Courtesy Jack McDonald.*

Below: The sight of Munger Hall and the boisterous Wellesley College women fills runners—both the fast and the slow—with overwhelming support as they begin to approach the halfway mark. *Photo by Paul C. Clerici.*

with great affection as the Scream Tunnel. To the uninitiated, the sound can be unnerving. To the veteran, it is invigorating.

In the beginning, according to the school, Wellesley College students were at that first Boston race in 1897 to cheer on an area runner. Since then, the support, the volume, and the excitement have grown exponentially.

When women were officially allowed to run the Boston Marathon in 1972, the level of love exploded to the point where nearly five hundred yards of thousands of Blue gather at the 20K mark (12.43 miles) in the shadow of Munger Hall and stretch over the metal barricades to high-five runners, cheer even louder, and offer and—more often than not—receive kisses. The Munger student residents who organize this massive boost of prolonged energy even create personal posters of support for the athletes whose family members or friends (or the runners themselves) contact them beforehand.

The Tunnel can be a blessing or a curse, depending on a runner's state of mind. The blessing of the tremendous vocal support is that it can reawaken a runner who might need the boost; it can be a curse if a runner allows that volume to overtake his or her stride, form, and pace.

Either way, the Wellesley College women fill runners with the passion and support rarely seen elsewhere, so much so that at the 1992 Boston Marathon, eventual victor Ibrahim Hussein of Kenya—a three-time Boston winner (1988, 1991, 1992) and international marathoner—smilingly blocked his ears with his hands as he ran by with great appreciation.

"Oh!" Squires exclaimed at the mention of the Wellesley College women. "They've got flowers, signs. The noise! They scream and yell. And if you are a Boston person with something on that says Boston, they'll scream and yell even more. But relax. Enjoy it. Relax your face and smile. You want to try and relax your face because that relaxes your neck and so on. Run relaxed."

Shortly after Wellesley College is Wellesley Center. Welcome to the halfway point of the Boston Marathon! Well, sort of.

Wellesley is indeed the home of the 13.1-mile mark, the half marathon, the 21K. But it is not really halfway in regard to the effort and struggle required in a marathon.

"That's at 20 [miles]," Squires said with great conviction. "Ignore the half [as a midway point]. Just keep going. Go with the flow. But change gears. You're dong the same thing for so long that you've gotta change gears. You stretch your legs out."

Within the Natick and Newton town borders of Wellesley, the course dips from 170 feet to 53 feet, but that includes several rises and falls that begin to torture the legs. Runners enter Wellesley on a 48-foot decline, followed

Wellesley Town Center includes the Mile 13 marker (near the clock at right) and the halfway point of 13.1 miles. *Photo by Paul C. Clerici.*

by a slight uptick before another 12-foot dip, a 28-foot incline and, finally, another decline. This is a significant point to remember because this leads to the demanding miles of Newton, which begin with a 111-foot drop when entering the town.

"Pay attention," Squires cautions runners about the course between miles fourteen and fifteen. "You're going to roll downhill. This is the first big one. Not the Newton hills but the Wellesley hills—good ones. This one works your quads, so loosen your shoulders up. Drop your arms and shoulders, and as you go down, shake a little, too. What you're doing is you're telling your muscles that moving back and forth that it's fine. You're going to need your arms ready."

The steep decline is where Squires famously tested a tangent theory of his for his athletes. He recalls that on an early Sunday morning, with tennis ball in hand, "I wanted to prove a point that they don't understand—that they have to go to the left side or the right side of the street. They wanted to go in the middle of the road, but sometimes the middle has a crown, and it's the highest point. So I took the ball and let it go, and it followed that path to the right and eventually to the curb. I proved that that was where you should run, not the middle of the street. You want to see it. After a while, you can train your eyes to look over and see where to go that's flat and shorter."

Common sights associated with the Boston Marathon include portable toilets, tents, and signs, some of which are whimsically personalized, such as this "No Stopping Monday" sign with a runner breaking the tape. *Photo by Paul C. Clerici.*

Despite being only halfway to Boston—and a point in the race when most runners monitor their half-marathon splits—Wellesley has actually been where many elites have begun their winning push.

In 1901, on his way to becoming the first winner to successfully defend his title, John P. Caffery passed the leader around Wellesley Square to win in 2:29:23. The following year in Wellesley, although a bit earlier, Samuel A. Mellor Jr. of New York made his move to victory in the 1902 Boston Marathon. William "Bill" Kennedy, nicknamed "Bricklayer" due to his New York occupation, charged ahead in Wellesley (and later in Newton Lower

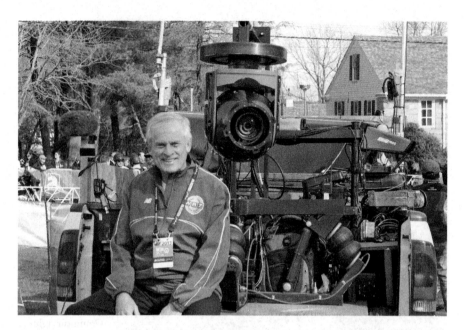

Former Boston Marathon race director Tim Kilduff, co-founder of the Spotters Network (a system of race-time data collection and distribution for live television coverage), sits on the lead vehicle from which he commentates during the race for the local TV station's live wire-to-wire programming. Above his left shoulder is the gyroscope television camera that provides the steady visuals of the lead men. *Courtesy Tim Kilduff.*

Falls) to win the twenty-first running in 1917. And Jerome Drayton of Canada created his own separation after the Wellesley hills on his way to winning the 1977 Boston Marathon.

In 2007, when NASA astronaut and Massachusetts native Suni Williams ran the Boston Marathon in space on the ISS, several of her friends and family members cheered on other marathoners in Wellesley at the fourteen-mile mark in acknowledgment of her Expedition 14, which was also represented by the bib number 14000 that she was given to wear by the BAA.

Wellesley—which is basically split between Central Street on Route 135 and Washington Street on Route 16—features 4.21 miles of the race before the fun begins in Newton, Brighton, Brookline, and Boston.

CHAPTER 7

NEWTON:

MILES 15.93 TO 21.35

Nearly 100 years after the birth of the United States of America—97, to be exact—the city of Newton was officially designated as such in 1873. Prior to that, this parcel of land was part of Cambridge, which had received it from Watertown in 1633. Over the ensuing centuries, it was known as Cambridge Village in 1688, Newtown in 1691, Newton in 1766, and, finally, the city of Newton 107 years later.

The origin of the name Newton can most likely be traced to a common description of that particular part of land. According to the Massachusetts Secretary of the Commonwealth Division of Public Records, the first reference of the lowercase "newe town" was listed in state records on July 26, 1631, followed within the next several years as Newe Towne in 1632, and Newetowne (or Newtown, as some would drop the last letter) in 1638.

Newton is composed of the separate and distinct villages of Auburndale, Chestnut Hill, Newton Centre, Newton Corner, Newton Highlands, Newton Lower Falls, Newton Upper Falls, Newtonville, Nonantum, Oak Hill, Waban, and West Newton, through only some of which marathoners will run.

To some (or most), the Boston Marathon begins in Newton.

As runners turn slightly into Newton Lower Falls at the Charles River and the town line at 15.93 miles (for runners who are unsure of their whereabouts at this point, to their right can clearly be seen a building with Lower Falls Wine Co. spelled out on the side), the road continues to drop from about 150 feet at 15.5 miles in Wellesley to about 50 just before 16.0 miles in Newton.

Longtime Boston Marathon race official John "Jock" Semple (14) and fellow Boston Athletic Association teammate Charlie "Doc" Robbins (18) run through the Newton hills in the forty-seventh edition of the Boston Marathon in 1943. Semple came in thirteenth (2:52:10) and Robbins in fourteenth (2:52:17). *Courtesy RunningPast.com.*

Upon seeing the Entering Newton sign, runners will soon approach the Mile 16 marker just ahead, the Route 128/95 overpass hill, and, soon, the Newton hills. *Photo by Paul C. Clerici.*

The Newton Lower Falls section is also where several eventual wins were decided, even with about ten miles remaining (depending on the year and the start location). It was in this area where CR holder Les Pawson (2:31:01 in 1933) battled the heat and a few top runners in 1938—including Johnny "The Elder" Kelley, Clarence DeMar, and Gerard Cote—and began to own the lead en route to his second of three wins.

As for visuals to get the runners prepared to hunker down for the bulk of the course's landmark hurdles, there are the brightly colored Federal Colonial historic Reverend Alfred Louis Baury House on the left, the sixteen-mile mark to the right, and the ominous-looking Route 128/95 Yankee Division Highway overpass straight ahead.

"It's a killer," said Squires of the terrain.

While thankfully not a permanent landmark hurdle, it was on the course in Newton where Yun Bok Suh, on his way to a WR victory in the 1947 Boston Marathon, tripped and fell over a fox terrier dog with no sense of propriety. Yun Bok Suh's 2:25:39 is the first and, to date, only men's WR.

In the 1961 race, perhaps jealous of the terrier's brief fame in the spotlight, a black dog this time took down the BAA's only Boston Marathon winner, Johnny "The Younger" Kelley, who won in 1957. The Connecticut native resumed his push for a second win but recorded his fourth runner-up finish in six years.

Also in the Newton area, Penti Rummakko of Finland in the 1969 Boston Marathon was on the receiving end of an unsolicited and unprovoked attack by a spectator, whose rage seemed to affect the Fin, who finished in tenth place.

As runners struggle (or not) up and over the approximate 150-yard roadway incline of about eighty feet of elevation, the supportive sounds of honking horns from cars below on the highway can be just the encouragement they need to overcome the overpass. Even drivers traveling over seventy miles per hour support the runners!

"It's like a rollercoaster. You go down the darn thing like a rollercoaster, and then you go right up," Squires described of the hill. "That's a good name. You should name it Rollercoaster Hill. It's a bitch! And then there's Hospital Hill, the little one."

According to the BAA, this area within the next mile or so—from the dips of Newton Lower Falls at around sixteen miles to the Newton-Wellesley Hospital and the Woodland Country Club golf course at seventeen miles—is where the most people drop out of the Boston Marathon.

Due to a confluence of circumstances—tortuous, unrelenting ups and downs from Newton Lower Falls and the overpass; possible less-than-ideal winter training taking its toll; the welcoming Newton-Wellesley Hospital at about 16.5 miles; and the easy accessibility of the Woodland MBTA train station stop to the right of the runners, just feet from the course—doubt can easily enter the mind of a marathoner with second thoughts or injuries. But a huge boost can also fill the runner who passes by such temptations.

"If it's a hot day, you're going to get a good cool breeze from all those cars that are coming by. It's wide open. But that's only going to be for about eighty to one hundred yards," Squires said of the highway traffic below the course. "It's a time that you want to use your new muscles. You used some muscles going down those hills—now use your new muscles going up these hills. See, this is the worst downhill. You have to think, and you have to work physically here."

Squires further instructs, "Take shorter strides and use good arm swings, and relax your arms. Look, arms only weigh four, maybe five pounds. Just think, think, think—[let them] pull you up the hill. Have them a little bit lower."

Slyly, the overpass incline actually continues to the set of traffic lights at the corner of Washington Street and Beacon Street (which bisects from the right of the runners). It's not until runners reach the lights and then turn left—still on Washington—that gravity comes to help and runners pass by the hospital and the Temple Reyim on the right.

"When you get to the set of lights, know that you're going to have three small downhills. People don't realize that, but I do. I've analyzed it," Squires said with confidence. "The very first one is the minute you get over that hill at the lights, then with the hospital on your right, and then at the [Woodland] T station. Use the flats between."

Mile 17, across from the golf course, offers a brief respite to recover on Washington before the exciting, scary, loud and sharp right-hand turn onto Commonwealth Avenue at 17.4 miles where the West Newton Fire Department Station 2 is located.

It was also in this area of Auburndale in 1949 that eventual winner Karl Gosta Leandersson of Sweden almost didn't make it to the Commonwealth Avenue turn. With less than ten miles to go, a wayward vehicle nearly hit him on the course. Fortunately, he went on to win. And he became the first and, to date, only Boston Marathon champion from his country.

The drastic eastward direction can also bring on a wind and temperature change from the distant Atlantic Ocean as marathoners begin to run toward Boston. But the crowd support at the bend is phenomenal—a wall of color and sound! From this spot, the next four miles contain the notorious Newton hills and Heartbreak Hill.

The famous—and to some, daunting—right-hand turn onto Commonwealth Avenue at the West Newton Fire Department Station 2 and the start of the Newton hills. *Photo by Paul C. Clerici.*

"Going to the fire station should be recovery. The minute you hit the fire station, there's a little roll of no more than fifty to sixty yards before what I call Fire Station Hill, and that's where you should do your first surge, your first pickup," Squires said of what will loosen up the legs and prepare them for the succession of obstacles.

While no single hill is insurmountable on its own, it is the location of each on the course and their proximity to each other that matters. Having four hills undulate between about 17.5 and 21.5 miles is not where a marathoner wants to see such challenges.

"Strategy starts from the fire station to the finish," Squires said of the final nine miles, adding that this is true whether the runner is an elite racer, age-grouper, or average marathoner. "That's the place where you're going to have to make a decision. 'Am I going to stay with this group?' 'Am I going to leave this group and move into another group?' 'Am I just going to do a pickup and get out of a group?' 'Am I going to go it alone?' This is when you decide."

The keys to running the Newton hills? "Run the flats, tilt into the hills slightly and run through them when you get to the top," Squires said. "The first fifteen miles, you've taken the same stride length, fairly close. Now what you have with these hills…they're giving you a way to rest—shorten your stride. That's good. You can relax your leg muscles, but your arms are going to do more work. You're swinging them more, and you're going to make sure that as they do, you can feel them relaxed. And don't squeeze your hands. Relax."

There are technically two Commonwealth Avenue roads parallel to each other, as a grass median separates a predominantly one-way access road to the left of the runners from the Route 30 two-way roadway of the Boston Marathon course. On nearly every day other than Patriots' Day, the access road is utilized heavily as a training run for athletes of all abilities and goals. On some weekends, there are so many people running that it can easily resemble the field of a good-size road race.

"The first hill is the shortest and probably the easiest of the marathon hills. Take it gradual because you just came off a hill," said Squires of the first hill immediately after the fire station. "When it gets up there and then goes down gradually—probably another twenty-five to thirty yards—that's the time to work your way into a good mile. Push it hard. You're pushing, but you're trying to think form—like you're becoming a track runner in that you think like a one-minute run, three-minute rest, two-minute run, three-minute rest and then one more. Three little strides that'll stretch your muscles out and get your arms in good form. That's what I'd tell my guys."

The eighteen-mile mark is on Commonwealth at Exeter Street, a steady incline. This is when a runner's legs are (hopefully) beginning to respond from the previous leg actions. And as with most of Commonwealth, the spectators carry the runners. And it is the wise marathoner who refrains from the occasional offer of beer or a hot dog.

Just after nineteen miles, on the right-hand side of the runners, is Newton City Hall. About a tenth of a mile ahead, to the left of the runners, at the corner of Walnut Street, is the Rich Muno–created *Young at Heart* statue of Johnny "The Elder" Kelley. On the day before the 1993 Boston Marathon, on the side of Walnut opposite the statue, a ceremonial unveiling was held.

Johnny "The Elder" Kelley, who was a two-time U.S. Olympian (1936, 1948), two-time Boston winner (1935, 1945), and seven-time Boston runner-up who started a record sixty-one Bostons and finished a record fifty-eight, actually dropped out of his first two attempts in 1928 and 1932. So revered and respected was the nonagenarian, who in 2000 was named "Runner of the Century" by *Runner's World* magazine, that even though two-time defending champion Ibrahim Hussein was to compete the day after the statue unveiling, the Kenyan came out to be part of the festivities.

When it was dedicated, the statue—which depicts a twenty-seven-year-old Kelley winning the 1935 Boston Marathon holding hands with an

The *Young at Heart* statue of Johnny "The Elder" Kelley is located to the left of the runners just after nineteen miles and before yet another hill. *Photo by Paul C. Clerici.*

The steady incline of Heartbreak Hill, which occurs shortly after twenty miles in Newton, can be a place of great support with throngs of spectators or a lonely no-man's land toward the end, when only a few neighbors stay to cheer. *Photo by Paul C. Clerici.*

eighty-three-year-old Kelley finishing the 1991 Boston—faced the oncoming runners. However, shortly thereafter, a car accident slightly damaged the statue, which was then moved across Walnut Street and adjusted to face the same direction as the runners, who must crane their neck back to the left if they wish to see the bronze piece of art while they run the Boston Marathon. It had been decided that it'd be fitting to have ol' Johnny face the direction of the impending upcoming Heartbreak Hill, whose name has its ties to the late champion (he was ninety-seven when he died in 2004).

From Walnut Street, a longer hill can be seen. It grows steadily from *Young at Heart* for just under half a mile at a climb of about one hundred feet.

"This is slightly shorter than Heartbreak Hill in length, and when you finish this hill, it should tell you that you're within yourself because it's almost like Heartbreak Hill and you've done it," said Squires. "Relax over it. Shorten the strides and swing the arms. Relax."

And despite the playful scenes of parties, inflatable modular moon walks, and barbecues at and around the twenty-mile mark, where spectators continue to cheer and support the plight of the runners, the task at hand is serious. This nondescript paved landmark—stretching about a half mile from Centre Street to Hammond Street near Boston College at a climb of about 650 yards—is Heartbreak Hill.

Longtime *Boston Globe* sports editor Jerry Nason is credited with coining the name when he covered the 1936 Boston Marathon and observed defending champion Kelley's remarkable comeback over the Newton hills to catch Ellison "Tarzan" Brown, a Narragansett Rhode Island Indian, at BC. At the moment the two were running next to each other, Nason reported that Kelley patted Brown on the back in a sign of acknowledgement, which would presumably be followed by Kelley continuing his momentum to take the lead (which he would later admit he should have done). Instead, Kelley did not excel past, and Brown received a jolt from the contact and charged out to an eventual 2:33:40 win, with Kelley finishing a disappointing fifth. In Nason's description, he would say that it broke Johnny's heart. The phrase Heartbreak Hill would eventually become a reference to the fourth and final hill in Newton, breaking many hearts in the ensuing years.

There is a way to prepare for Heartbreak Hill, of course. When runners approach the intersection of Centre Street, they take notice of what's ahead just after the twenty-mile mark near Sumner Street.

"Between nineteen and twenty, don't fight the hills," Squires says regarding the approximate mile from Newton City Hall to the climb shortly after Centre. "You've got flat before it, and then you hit the stores, and that's telling you

So talented was Joan Benoit Samuelson (shown here in the 1989 Boston Marathon, in which she came in as the ninth woman) that she famously wondered while running Boston in 1979 about the whereabouts of Heartbreak Hill only to find out it was just about behind her. The Maine native won her debut Boston in an American and course record 2:35:15. She would also win Boston in 1983 in a course, American, and world record 2:22:43, as well as the Olympic Marathon gold medal in 1984. *Photo by Leo Kulinski Jr.*

from the light to the light is six hundred yards. It goes up so gradually at that light, and then you know. But you can rest on hills—that's a rest phase. You're using four times your body mass to push you up a hill, so you want that shorter stride so you can get more muscle mass and power into it to take you up."

And the downhill? "The tendency is the ol' elephant feet—boom, boom, boom—as you land hard. Don't do that. Don't think you're stretching your legs out as you go down. Tilt forward, drop your arms and use your own momentum. You don't want to go down like a madman. Let it flow."

Heartbreak Hill is also the site where many a Boston Marathon has been—and presumably will be—decided. Johnny Miles in 1926 made his move on this hill to eventually win the first of his two Boston titles.

Left: With the Boston Marathon on the international elites' calendar after prize money began to be awarded, showdowns such as this one in 1989 between eventual winner Abebe Mekonnen of Ethiopia (4) and runner-up Juma Ikangaa of Tanzania (2) became expected and welcomed. *Photo by Leo Kulinski Jr.*

Below: A sight for sore eyes—and legs—is the Mile 21 marker (right) and the Gothic steeples of Gasson Hall on the campus of Boston College, which is also the crest of Heartbreak Hill. *Photo by Paul C. Clerici.*

With a presumably large enough lead on Heartbreak, Bill Rodgers in 1975 stopped the first of five separate instances to drink some water. He did likewise to tie his shoes and drink more water en route to a 2:09:55 win in an American record (AR) and CR. This was also the first of his four Boston wins.

In 1990, Gelindo Bordin utilized the hills to reel in Juma Ikangaa of Tanzania on his way to becoming the first Olympic men's marathon winner to also win the Boston Marathon, joining Joan Benoit Samuelson, Rosa Mota, and Fatuma Roba as the only four athletes to win both titles.

"The last two hills are the hurting hills because they're packed together, and it seems like you never get to Heartbreak Hill. That stretch [between them] seems to last forever," said Squires. "Stay with the shorter stride and use more arms. Still. It works. And know that it's sharp, but it's over quick, and then it's a fake and you have about two hundred yards before you get another one—on the same hill! And run through the hills. Don't race a hill. You can't beat a hill—you'll lose every time. You can run a hill. There's a difference. You can run the hills and then race the flats in between in short bursts to stretch your legs out. Get the blood to flow freely—it's been all cramped up."

Squires adds, "If you do the right things, you'll be okay."

But there are times when that fails. "Be careful what you drink there," he said with caution and amusement. "One year when I ran, I grabbed a cup some kids gave me. I took a big drink, and it was, if I remember, a 7 and 7 [a highball cocktail of Seagram's Seven Crown whiskey and 7 Up soft drink]. I spent the next mile trying to spit it out and wipe the taste off my tongue."

At the end of Heartbreak Hill, when runners finally raise their heads high, can be seen the majestic stone Gothic steeples of Gasson Hall on the campus of BC, just after the twenty-one-mile mark.

Thanks to transferred Maryland Province of the Society of Jesus Father John McElroy, S.J., who gifted land to the trustees of Boston College in 1863 (twenty years after he had contacted Jesuit Bishop of Boston Benedict Joseph Fenwick, S.J., to no avail), Jesuit priests of the order of the Society of Jesus were able to found BC in the South End neighborhood of Boston. In 1909, ground was broken in its current Chestnut Hill location on the former farmland of Adams Amos Lawrence. Four years later, the first building erected on campus was the Recitation Building, which can be seen from the Boston Marathon course as Gasson Hall, so named after its president at the time, Thomas I. Gasson, S.J.

Bill Rodgers often used a relentless jab of surges over the Newton hills to fell his victims, but he has also succumbed. He has said—half jokingly—that

Above: At the base of a sharp post–Heartbreak Hill downhill is the "Welcome to Brighton" sign (left), which notifies marathoners they have entered this neighborhood of Boston, with Boston College still to the right. *Photo by Paul C. Clerici.*

Left: Ingrid Kristiansen of Norway, shown here winning the 1989 Boston Marathon, also won in the first year prize money was awarded (1986). *Photo by Leo Kulinski Jr.*

his "favorite" dropout spot is the crest of Heartbreak, within the comfort of the Gasson towers and an aid station.

In 1926, Albin Stenroos of Finland was in the lead until BC, when Johnny Miles took over and continued to his CR win in 2:25:40 (he would win again in 1929). In 1953, Karl Gosta Leandersson thought he was on his way to win number two, but Keizo Yamada of Japan broke away from him and Veikko Karvonen of Finland at BC to win in a time of 2:18:51.

BC was also the site where two Fins made their moves to victory ten years apart: Eino Oksanen, who in 1962 won his third title, and Olavi Suomalainen, who won his first in '72. And Greg Meyer utilized his Newton hill training to win the 1983 Boston Marathon, to date the last American to win the men's race.

Catherine Ndereba—"Catherine the Great"—won her fourth and second consecutive title in 2005, when she clawed back from certain defeat to pass her final foe atop Heartbreak Hill in an eventual 110-second cushion to victory.

At the top of Heartbreak Hill was also where fans, spectators, participants, and the media witnessed an example of the brotherhood of athletes. During the 1978 Boston Marathon, Bill Rodgers—wearing his golden yellow store logo singlet and number-three bib—tapped the shoulder of Bob Hall in a congratulatory manner as he ran past on his way to his second win, eliciting a cheer from the two-time national wheelchair champion. It was a pure athlete-to-athlete gesture.

The reward of reaching BC is cautionary: Heartbreak Hill is finished, and there is a very short flatland that allows the legs a slight bit of a rest, but that is quickly followed by a jarring and potentially dangerous downhill to the Brighton neighborhood of Boston (still at BC).

There is a tendency for runners to let it fly to the Lake Street intersection—where the MBTA train begins its Boston College Green Line service—as some kind of treat for surviving the hills. But take heed. "Let the hill pull you down all the way to Lake Street," cautions Squires. "Some runners think that's it, that the hills are done. I'll clue ya—you've got five to go. Five more miles. There are a lot of people that are in whackland when they get into the last four miles because they're on fumes. With the trained athletes, that's the strategy part [that comes into play]."

Of the eight towns and cities of the Boston Marathon course, Newton, at 5.42, features the most mileage.

CHAPTER 8

BRIGHTON/BROOKLINE: MILES 21.35 TO 24.70

While still on Commonwealth Avenue at BC, runners exit Newton into the Boston neighborhood of Brighton.

Until it became an official neighborhood of Boston in 1874, Brighton, whose namesake is presumably in England, was originally part of Cambridge and Little Cambridge. It is often colloquially referred to as Brighton-Allston or Allston-Brighton in connection with the next-door neighborhood of Allston, whose land was known as the Cambridge Crossing area of Brighton and in 1868 was so renamed in honor of South Carolina painter Washington Allston. The artist, who eventually lived in Cambridgeport and whose residential ties to Brighton came via the town's origins in Cambridge, was also honored when his name graced the local post office.

Brighton begins just prior to Lake Street, which is to the left of the runners. To the right is the St. Ignatius Church of Loyola, which while located on the BC campus since its dedication in 1949 is neither the church of nor the recipient of operating funds from Boston College.

In 2013, St. Ignatius served as a safe haven in the immediate aftermath of the bombings that occurred at and near the finish line of the Boston Marathon. When runners were stopped from proceeding in the race (as a safety measure, since it was unknown at the time whether or not there were additional bombs along the course), those in this area took refuge on the campus of the BC Eagles and in the church. Some runners were hours away from connecting with families and traveling home, largely due to suddenly being five miles from the finish and also because cellphone service was shut down by law enforcement as a precautionary measure.

Students, university personnel, and Jesuits alike provided water and sports drinks, food, phones and charges, medical assistance, and even interpreters (for foreign-language runners) to comfort those hundreds of stranded marathoners.

It took several hours for some people to contact family and friends and then organize transportation. State police updated people of the ongoing status, and BAA volunteers were also on hand to check the runners in and out of the church and also record whether or not they would take the provided buses and shuttles to the relocation area that had been set up at the Boston Common or return home.

In 1922, eleven years after his first win, Clarence DeMar pushed down Commonwealth Avenue toward Lake Street and passed leader James Henigan, who stopped at BC with an injury. This marked DeMar's second win, the beginning of a three-peat and the first of six victories in the next nine years.

To the left of the runners, just after Lake Street and slightly hidden behind a row of trees on the other side on Commonwealth, is the former site of the Cardinal's Residence, where the archbishop of Boston lived until Sean Patrick O'Malley was so appointed. Shortly thereafter, it was sold to BC. It is also the site of the Chancery and St. John's Seminary of the Archdiocese of Boston. The close relationship between Boston College and the archdiocese dates back to when both institutions were neighbors in the South End neighborhood of Boston before moving to the Chestnut Hill/Newton area in the early 1900s.

Runners continue in Brighton for only 1.10 miles—from miles 21.35 to 22.45—which includes a stretch of potential uncertainty near Evergreen Cemetery (twenty acres of the former Aspinwall Woods that was bought in 1848 and consecrated two years later) and the Chestnut Hill Reservoir (built between 1866–70, this portion is the former Nathaniel J. Bradlee Basin) to their right. This short piece of road that is known by many names—Haunted Mile, Cemetery Mile, Cemetery Mile of Lost Hope, to name a few—is where runners can finally process a body check after all the hills and damage to their legs.

It is also where, in 1897, John J. McDermott, the marathon's inaugural winner, first stopped to walk. A cramp in his left leg forced him to stop a couple more times in this general area, but after having his leg rubbed, he continued on to victory—even with another short stoppage on Beacon Street.

With the street-level T riding alongside the course to the left of the runners, temptation can appear every time a train passes by. While some do drop out at this point, solace can be taken that there are about twenty-two miles behind and but four ahead.

"The minute you see the cemetery, you're doing the baby rollercoaster all the way to the finish line. It rolls and rolls. If you've got anything in your tank, all you do is take it in," said Squires.

In the 1905 Boston Marathon, it was around the twenty-mile mark that a marathon cheater made his main victorious move to the podium. Well, technically, he was accused of cheating. In the 1904 Olympic Games Marathon in St. Louis, Frederick Lorz of New York dropped out of the race, rode in a car to the finish area and ended up "winning." Although he claimed humor as the reason for running back in the race, he was nevertheless disqualified.

In Boston, on the heels of a pair of top-five finishes (fourth in 1903, fifth in 1904), Frederick Lorz overtook the leader with about five miles remaining to finally win the 1905 Boston Marathon. However, it wasn't smooth sailing, as perhaps the mythical forces of the Olympic gods descended on the course in the form of two fallen bicyclists before him. He was able to jump over one, but the other knocked him down at the finish.

Just after the twenty-two-mile mark at Chestnut Hill Driveway, the course veers right onto Chestnut Hill Avenue and continues downhill to Cleveland Circle. The avenue dip takes a sharp left-hand turn—just past the site where the Bill Rodgers Running Center once stood—onto Beacon Street near the local athletic governing body office of the USA Track & Field–New England (USATF-NE) to the right.

For those new to town, Cleveland Circle is neither a rotary nor a roundabout. While there are a number of streets that meet at this one juncture—including Chestnut Hill Avenue, Sutherland Avenue (eventually), and Beacon Street—several sets of traffic lights orchestrate the vehicular flow.

Documents that describe the development of this area prior to 1870 are apparently lost to the sands of history. But what was once known as the higher-class residential Cleveland Circle–Englewood Area was also part of a larger tract called Aberdeen, named after the 1890 Aberdeen Land Company, whose namesake can be found in Scotland.

This area can be tricky, as the left-hand turn is sharp and sudden after the short downhill. At that tantalizing tangent, 1978 Boston Marathon wheelchair winner George Murray in 1980 enjoyed a mile lead when his wheel dipped into one of the T's street-level tracks and forced him to stop for repairs (he finished in eighth, but he would win again in 1985). And going for

Jean Driscoll, whose wheel once caught the railway tracks at Cleveland Circle in 1997, has the most wins in the women's wheelchair division with eight, including seven in a row from 1990 to 1996. *Courtesy* New England Runner.

Patti (Lyons) (Catalano) Dillon, running here in Amherst in 1984, was a runner-up in the Boston Marathon three times, one of which can be credited with an assist to a police horse, into whose hindquarters she ran in 1981. *Photo by Leo Kulinski Jr.*

an unprecedented eighth consecutive win in 1997, Jean Driscoll also caught a wheel on the track as she attempted to pass the leader. The damage to her wheelchair cost her enough time to come in second. Her victory three years later, in 2000, gave her that eighth and, at the time, record-setting title as the Boston Marathon athlete with the most wins.

In 1981, before the days when police barricades created a safe and wide running lane, spectators lined the streets and were within arm's length of the runners. Hundreds of enthusiastic people were held back by police officers and their horses—real ones, not those wooden DPW horses often used at construction sites. Local favorite Patti (Lyons) (Catalano) Dillon of

Shortly after runners turn left and depart Cleveland Circle, they reach the Brookline town line and the seemingly endless miles of Beacon Street. *Photo by Paul C. Clerici.*

Massachusetts, on the heels of two straight second-place showings in 1979 and 1980, was in the lead near the bend at Beacon Street in Cleveland Circle. As she was rounding that left-hand turn, she smacked right into the hindquarters of a fidgeting police horse that was trying to gain some footing on the train tracks while keeping order. The collision knocked her into her fellow runners. She was able to maintain her upright position, but eventual winner Allison Roe of New Zealand passed by her, causing the Bay Stater to come in second place for the third consecutive time (but in an AR 2:27:51).

"Just be alert," warned Squires. "It can also be dangerous on a wet day from snow or rain. You've got to put it down; you've got to watch those tracks. Those tracks are dangerous. I've seen people fall there."

Cleveland Circle is where Boston's second winner, Ronald J. MacDonald, dropped out of the 1901 race. Thirty-three years later, Johnny "The Elder" Kelley was in the midst of a possible victory against Dave Komonen of Canada until the American failed to match Komonen's winning pace (Kelley came in second but won the following year). Cleveland Circle is also where Kenyan Joseph Chebet in 1999 caught up to and passed the leader en route to a 2:09:52 win after having come in second the year before.

Once on Beacon, runners quickly cross into Brookline at 22.45 miles. Seventy-five years after being a part of Boston, the town of Brookline was incorporated in 1705—seventy-one years before the birth of the United States. It is a town rich with history, goods, people, and places. And just about a half mile north of the twenty-four-mile mark of the Boston Marathon is the home where President John F. Kennedy was born.

The Beacon Street miles in Brookline seem endless, especially with the number of rolling hills along the way.

"Just go with the flow. Don't over-stride it. From Brookline, you've got four small hills and one long downhill for about 150 yards," said Squires of this roadway. "But just go with it."

There can be a mental letdown along Beacon, as the major landmarks and highlights of the course—the euphoria of the start and early miles, Natick center, the cheering/kissing women at Wellesley College, Heartbreak Hill, Boston College, and Cleveland Circle—are behind the runners. But let Beacon occupy your attention, and these final miles will be rewarding.

Runners can watch the T continue its rounds to the left; wave at the students, residents, and visitors in the apartments and stores to the right that are mere yards from the course. And keep in mind that the longer it takes a runner to reach this point in the race, the longer those people have been on the sidewalks and yelling at the top of their lungs for each marathoner to make it to Boston.

At the twenty-three-mile mark at Winthrop Road, Beacon begins to dip toward Washington Square, which is two blocks ahead at Washington Street and marked by the beautiful eighteen-foot Victorian four-sided clock to the left of the runners (those paying close attention—and with real fine eyesight—can read Washington Square on its faces).

About a block and half before the twenty-four-mile mark at Charles Street is Coolidge Corner, the Brookline neighborhood so distinguished by the hundreds of cheering spectators at Harvard Street and the wonderful hidden jewel of shops, eateries, and culture. Another marker is the perfectly situated 1897 Tudor-style S.S. Pierce Building and its clock tower to the left that overlooks the intersection. It was at this corner of Beacon and Harvard in 1857 that Coolidge and Griggs family members built a general store, half of which bears the area's namesake.

It is also around this point in the race when runners begin—or continue—to badmouth King Edward VII for this extra mileage because it is here, right around twenty-four miles, of course, that many are reminded that this distance is so cherished for anyone who has run 26.2.

In the year of the 1980 Moscow Olympic boycott, outspoken champion Bill Rodgers, pictured here receiving water from legendary coach Bill Squires, ran the Boston Marathon with a death threat upon him that said he would not make it past twenty-four miles. *Jeff Johnson photo courtesy Bill Squires.*

Washington Square on Beacon Street is at the Mile 23 marker (right), as is another slight downhill. *Photo by Paul C. Clerici.*

"Yeah," Squires says with a chuckle, "this is long enough as it is! Remember, those older guys [in the early years] ran a mile and three quarters less than you. And this is also when you start to feel it, when you notice it."

Within the approximate miles of Brighton and Brookline are where several strategic and/or fortunate moves were made to victory in the Boston Marathon.

On Beacon Street in the general area of Kent Street is about where Ronald J. MacDonald passed Hamilton Gray of New York in 1898 to win the second Boston Marathon and where, in 1903, John C. Lorden of Massachusetts beat a stellar field that included the previous three champions in Samuel A. Mellor Jr. (1902) and John P. Caffery (1900, 1901), as well as two future winners in Michael Spring of New York (1904) and Frederick Lorz (1905).

In the 1932 race, defending champion James Henigan was helpless to repeat as Paul De Bruyn of Germany sped by on Beacon to win in 2:33:36, the time adding insult to injury because it bested Henigan's winning 1931 time by a healthy 13:09.

In 1948, Gerard Cote—after some legendary sustained verbal and physical tussling with Ted Vogel of Massachusetts—separated himself within the last three miles to win his fourth Boston Marathon.

In 1951, nineteen-year-old Shigeki Tanaka became the first of eight winners from Japan when he made his move with about four miles remaining.

Ambrose "Amby" Burfoot of Connecticut pulled away within the last five miles to win the 1968 race, becoming the first U.S. runner to claim the title in nearly a dozen years. His coach, Johnny "The Younger" Kelley, had been the last to win in 1957.

While in the final throes of Brookline, a famous landmark begins to come into view up ahead. Simple eye contact with its giant red triangle and white square frame high above the streets can instantly fill ailing, struggling runners with enough joy and promise to propel them to the finish. Those with energy left in their legs and a spring in their steps can also receive a boost from its glow. Located at the 25.2-mark in Kenmore Square is the sought-after CITGO sign. Depending on the density of the Beacon Street trees that line the sidewalks and often reach over the roadway, the visibility to the sign may vary. But once in Boston, there is no mistake. It will appear larger than life!

Combined mileage in Brighton (1.10 miles) and Brookline (2.25 miles) is 3.35 miles.

CHAPTER 9

BOSTON:
MILES 24.70 TO 26.20

R unners step on the marathon's namesake at 24.70 miles for the remaining 2,640 yards.

Known first by the Native Americans as Shawmut, it was ten yeas after the Pilgrims departed England on the *Mayflower* and established their colony in Plymouth, Massachusetts, that the town of Boston was incorporated in 1630. Named after the Lincolnshire County hometown in England of some of the colonists, Boston was incorporated as a city in 1822. The Massachusetts state capital is also one of the oldest cities in the United States.

The city line on Beacon can be easily missed, but it is visible to the right of the runners at St. Mary's Street. On the same cement signpost are separate small black-and-white street signs for St. Mary's Street and Beacon Street, and above Beacon and parallel to the course is Boston Line.

Welcome to Boston! Again (remember Brighton?).

Lawrence Brignolia of Massachusetts received a terrible welcome to Boston when he ran the 1899 race, which featured gale-force winds. Coming off a fifth-place finish the year before in the second running, in the third annual marathon, Brignolia took the lead in Newton and was on his way to a smooth victory when, on Beacon near St. Mary's, he stumbled on a rock and fell. But he persevered and decided to run/walk his way to the win, which he did in 2:54:38.

The view from Beacon opens up here as there are fewer trees—if any, in spots—along the course. The vastness reveals to the left of the runners the two-tone steeple of the Ruggles Baptist Church, located next to the Church

Runners in the Boston Marathon finally enter Boston proper at this simple sign at 24.70 miles. *Photo by Paul C. Clerici.*

Atop this hill, which is the overpass of the Massachusetts Turnpike, is Mile 25. The Boston skyline and Fenway Park can be seen to the right, and the CITGO sign (top left) finally seems within reach. *Photo by Paul C. Clerici.*

of the Cross about two blocks into Boston at the intersection of Park Drive. Also coming into view more clearly is that CITGO sign, which notifies runners they are closing in on the final mile.

But not so fast—literally. A few blocks beyond the two churches and the "Welcome to Audubon Circle" sign to the left is the beginning of the approximately 150-yard mean hill over the Interstate 90 Massachusetts Turnpike (Mass Pike) and the twenty-five-mile mark, where it was believed that some of the road construction on this overpass shortened the Boston Marathon distance in the 1950s. This is also the location of the last water station on the course.

It's a good, steady hill on the overpass, but it also offers a real clear glimpse of the city skyline—the sixty-story John Hancock Tower, the fifty-two-story Prudential Tower, and even the thirty-six-story 111 Huntington Avenue building. And to the right of the runners can also be seen the exterior green façade of the oldest ballpark in Major League Baseball—Fenway Park, home of the Boston Red Sox since 1912.

"The big thing is, it's almost over," Squires says with a smile. "Don't forget—short strides, arms, relax. Do it!"

Just ahead is the Fenway-Kenmore section of Boston, named for the "fens" (a type of wetland in the area) and Kenmore Street (a former roadway in the former Governor Square that Mayor James Michael Curley officially changed to Kenmore Square in 1931).

As big as life, straight ahead as runners prepare to turn right from Beacon onto Commonwealth, is the CITGO sign. The huge 3,600-square-foot LED advertising sign some six stories above street level was originally built in 1940 atop the divisional offices of CITGO predecessor Cities Service. The current triangular logo replaced the original one in 1965 and has been a familiar sight that can be seen from the stands inside Fenway Park, the campus of nearby Boston University, and, of course, from various points along the Boston Marathon route.

To the right of the runners, at the right-hand turn into Kenmore Square, is the historic Boston Hotel Buckminster. Built the same year as the first running of the race with which the marathoners are nearly finished (1897), the six-story brick-and-stone triangular-shaped building at the corner of Beacon Street and Brookline Avenue seems to guide the runners into Kenmore Square. Past notables at the hotel have included the famous (musicians Louis Armstrong, Billie Holiday, and Sarah Vaughan, all of whom performed at the Buckminster at one time or another) and the infamous (Joseph "Sport" Sullivan, a local bookmaker/gambler, and

Arnold "Chick" Gandil, a Chicago White Sox ballplayer, both of whom, at the hotel, planned the fix of the 1919 World Series that would become known as the Black Sox Scandal).

Marathoners enter and run on the multicolored brick-laid Kenmore Square, which at one time was the muddy basin of the expansive Charles River. In the 1870s, this area—as well as others at various times, including the Back Bay—was filled in to create what is now this portion of Boston.

Depending on when runners pass through Kenmore Square, they could be treated to the roars and cheers of tens of thousands of Red Sox fans emptying out of Fenway Park from that morning's ballgame. The crowd support is earsplitting! The confluence of Brookline Avenue, Beacon Street, Commonwealth Avenue, and its Boston University inhabitants, Red Sox fans, bar and restaurant patrons, and Boston Marathon fans adds up to an experience not to be missed.

Once runners straighten out onto Commonwealth in Kenmore Square, painted on the road before them can be read the encouraging and rewarding words "One Mile to Go," and up ahead, like a gigantic otherworldly marker, is the John Hancock Tower beckoning marathoners to its finish line.

Catherine Ndereba in 2004 turned it on in Kenmore Square on her way to her third win in five years. In 2002, she had also finished in second place, as it took a 2:20:43 CR by Margaret Okayo of Kenya to knock off the two-time defending champion (Ndereba won in 2000 and 2001).

In the centennial edition of the Boston Marathon in 1996, Uta Pippig around the twenty-five-mile mark surged ahead to her three-peat after not only chasing down Tegla Loroupe of Kenya but doing so after suffering through severe internal pains and the corresponding second-place margin.

Just after 25.2 miles is the Kenmore Square T station to the right of the runners. Around this area is where it is believed that Rosie Ruiz reportedly slipped into the 1980 Boston Marathon and was soon treated as the winner of the women's race when she was the first female to cross the finish line—that is, until the BAA quickly investigated its suspicions and subsequently stripped her of the title and then awarded Canadian Jacqueline Gareau the mantle and medal of champion in a ceremony one week later.

There is a nice stretch of several flat blocks on which runners can both recover and rejoice. Crowd noise might interrupt any inner thoughts, but the wave of excitement and anticipation is intoxicating.

With five- to eight-story walls of windows, brick and stone to the right of the runners and the beginning of the Commonwealth Avenue Mall—a median of grass, trees and monuments that separates the east and west lanes

Catherine Ndereba, the first Kenyan woman to win the Boston Marathon (2000), holds the most titles in the women's open division, with four between 2000 and 2005. *Jonathan S. McElvery photo courtesy* New England Runner.

of Commonwealth Avenue's Route 2—to the left, marathoners will next run under the Charlesgate overpass and then over a Charles River waterway en route to Massachusetts Avenue and the Tommy Leonard Bridge in the shadow of the 1913 Harvard Club.

The bridge's namesake is the official greeter of the Boston Marathon and founder of the internationally renowned Falmouth Road Race in Cape Cod. The location of the bridge is fortuitous in that it is within a few yards of the Eliot Hotel, inside of which once housed the Eliot Lounge, the famous bar (of which he was the lead barkeep/organizer) that was the epicenter of all things running. The lounge was a meeting place before and after group runs; the site of packed Boston Marathon parties and gatherings of elite and amateur runners alike; and a local museum of photographs, artifacts, banners and flags representing road races, athletes, and countries.

There was also the "Walkway of the Running Stars" on the sidewalk outside the Eliot's doors that, at one time or another, featured the cemented esteemed footprints of marathoners Amby Burfoot, Patti Dillon, Johnny "The Elder" Kelley, Johnny "The Younger" Kelley, Bill Rodgers, Joan Benoit Samuelson, Geoff Smith, and Squires, among others, which included Leonard. The Eliot Lounge closed in 1996, and the footprints have since faded and been removed.

For most years in the Boston Marathon, runners continued straight ahead on Commonwealth, as the bisecting Massachusetts Avenue was closed to vehicular traffic. But in 2006, as a way to alleviate some of the city's marathon-related detoured traffic and inevitable backups along the many cow path–engineered roads, the course changed to turn slightly to the left and under the Tommy Leonard Bridge.

"That's a dip in the road!" acknowledged Squires of the short valley under the bridge. "It's the same yardage [as when the course stayed on Commonwealth], but if you're hurting, you can feel it. But it's over quick."

This enclave of Commonwealth, at the bridge, is also where in 2013, thousands of marathoners—after an initial number was redirected to continue on Commonwealth instead of turning up Hereford Street—were held up when the race was stopped after the two bombings occurred less than a half mile away on Boylston. The logjam reached as far back as Kenmore Square and beyond. Runners were initially unaware of the reason but then soon began to learn more and search for information. As at BC, nearby residents and spectators in this area also offered assistance to those unable to move onward.

The penultimate turn of the Boston Marathon is up ahead, seen almost immediately after resurfacing from under the bridge and back onto Commonwealth. A sharp right-hand turn onto Hereford Street is followed by a slight incline through tony Newbury Street and straight toward the John B. Hynes Memorial Convention Center, the location of most of the expos where runners picked up their bib numbers.

This short, approximately two-block-long incline is also where some elite runners make their move to victory. Alvaro Mejia of Colombia charged past Patrick McMahon of Ireland on Hereford to win in 1971. It is also where the leaders whip around the last corner to get to the final stretch at the sharp left-hand turn onto Boylston Street, revealing the promised land: three and a half blocks of sights and sounds formed by music, yells of

A sense of the magnitude of the Boston Marathon is evident as Johnny "The Younger" Kelley grinds it out past the old Exeter Street Theatre en route to a second-place showing in the 1963 race, with Brian Kilby of Great Britain on his heels. *Courtesy RunningPast.com.*

An aerial view of the final three-and-a-half-block Boylston Street portion of the Boston Marathon, from the Hereford Street turn (top left corner) to the finish line (bottom right corner). *Photo by Paul C. Clerici.*

thousands of spectators, balloons, banners, and all things celebratory within the thunderous cheers of the awaiting masses.

One of the most famous and exciting moments in Boston Marathon history took place over this last turn in 1982, when both Alberto Salazar and Dick Beardsley appeared on Boylston within arm's length of each other. From the Newton hills, the two duked it out to the point that nothing but a close finish would satisfy. The two-second CR win by Salazar in 2:08:52 capped off a day of monumental images that included top runners—such as four-time winner Bill Rodgers—who faded back due to the heat, Beardsley's quick damage control when he stepped into a pothole that seemed to relieve his muscle cramps, and several accompanying police motorcycles that appeared to impede the duo's progress. Also, for the first time, two runners (Salazar and Beardsley) turned in sub-2:09:00 times, and then there was Salazar's post-race multi-IV regimen. It certainly lived up to its moniker of the "Duel in the Sun."

This last turn onto Boylston is to be conquered, savored, and cherished. And runners even appear on a huge exterior monitor at the corner of Exeter Street that airs the television coverage.

On Boylston, just after Gloucester Street, is where the start line was located in 2008 for the U.S. Olympic Team Trials Women's Marathon that was held the day before the Boston race. Also, every Boston Marathon has finished within about a three-block span on or near Boylston (and some via Commonwealth Avenue).

To the right of the runners is the 1.3-acre Prudential Center South Garden, whose centerpiece is the five-ton, twenty-seven-foot *Quest Eternal* statue, which depicts a slightly contorted, muscular nude man whose left arm is reaching skyward. A cement and landscaped pedestrian plaza, this was once the location of Ring Road, which between 1965 and 1985 served as an access way parallel to Boylston and the finish line a few yards in front of the 1967 Donald DeLue bronze artwork (in its current form, Ring Road connects Boylston Street and Huntington Avenue).

In those twenty-one years, men's winners came from eight countries, including six from the United States—Amby Burfoot, Jon Anderson, Bill Rodgers (four), Jack Fultz, Alberto Salazar, and Greg Meyer—and back-to-back wins by Geoff Smith. This era also saw the first fourteen women's titles, which included nine American wins—Nina Kuscsik, Jacqueline Hansen, Miki Gorman (two), Kim Merritt, Gayle Barron, Joan Benoit Samuelson (two), and Lisa Larsen-Weidenbach—and a WR in 1975 by Liane Winter, as well as the first ten men's wheelchair competitions

The final Boylston Street stretch to the finish line passes by the Lenox Hotel at Exeter Street (left). Farther down Exeter, where the Boston Athletic Association's clubhouse was once located, is where the Boston Marathon finished from 1899 to 1964. *Photo by Frank Clerici Sr.*

(including five WR times and Bob Hall's groundbreaking 2:58:00 in 1975) and the first nine women's wheelchair races, which included four WR times and all American victors.

Another block and a half ahead is Exeter Street, where the former site of the BAA clubhouse (the southwest corner of the Boston Public Library) was located and where the finish line was situated from 1899 to 1964, just beyond the Exeter Street entrance of the 1900 Hotel Lenox.

Over those sixty-six years, at one time or another, the finish line was marked simply by an opposing pair of approximately eight-foot poles with a pennant at the top of each and the word "Finish" next to the BAA's unicorn logo and accompanied by police officers and suit-dressed race officials standing on the dirt road. There was also a thin finish-line tape through which winners would break. And when it was paved, the underlined word "Finish" was painted on the street. Eventually, crowd control, barricades, mounted police, and media bleachers were required.

In 1986, when the John Hancock Mutual Life Insurance Company signed on as the marathon's major sponsor, the finish line was understandably

In the shadow of the Boston Public Library, spectators applaud the runners—whether first or last. *Photo by Paul C. Clerici.*

moved from Ring Road and the shadow of the Prudential Tower—an insurance company competitor—closer to its own John Hancock Tower near the Boston Public Library. And a few blocks away, the first two races (1897 and 1898) finished at the long-gone BAA track on the Irvington Street Oval near Copley Square.

Since 1986, this final distance has seen numerous close finishes in which victory was not decided until the last few strides.

One of the first close calls was in 1988, when Ibrahim Hussein edged Juma Ikangaa by one second. The race was decided within the final one hundred yards.

From 2009 to 2012, the top prize was decided by mere seconds. In 2009, one second separated first and second place when Salina Kosgei of Kenya finally pulled away, with the course running out of land, to win in 2:32:16. Dire Tune of Ethiopia came in second at 2:32:17, and Kara Goucher of Oregon was third, just nine seconds behind Kosgei. The following year, Teyba Erkesso of Ethiopia kept herself ahead to win the 2010 Boston Marathon by three seconds over Tatyana Pushkareva of Russia.

And even though Geoffrey Mutai of Kenya ran a phenomenal world-best 2:03:02 in 2011, he was followed closely by fellow Kenyan Moses Mosop, the runner-up at 2:03:06! And Caroline Kilel of Kenya felt Desiree Davila

While the color, façade, and layout may change from time to time, the pageantry and excitement of the Boston Marathon finish remains constant. *Photo by Frank Clerici Sr.*

The evolving look of the Boston Marathon finish line is shown here with the Boston Athletic Association unicorn logo and its BAA initials in 1991, when Ibrahim Hussein of Kenya won the second of his three crowns. *Marshall Wolfe photo courtesy* New England Runner.

of Minnesota on her heels when, in that same year, she beat the American by only two seconds with a time of 2:22:36. That margin of victory was also what separated Sharon Cherop of Kenya in 2012 in her 2:31:50 win over fellow Kenyan Jemima Jelagat Sumgong.

Also of note on Boylston, of course, is the final mile marker—26 M—which is located at the end of the Pru's South Garden, about a block before a set of lights that manages no intersection (it's there to control traffic on Boylston at a parking garage entranceway and a crosswalk). Runners have 385 yards remaining to reach the world-famous finish line, which is framed on the left by dozens of country flags along the sidewalk; on the right by the loud and supportive yells and applause from bleacher sections of spectators, VIPs, and officials; above by the bridge of photographers and videographers; and on the street level by the wide and bright laminated finish-line mat.

Also within those final yards, runners will pass on their left two locations to remember: the Forum bar and restaurant (at the Ring Road set of lights about a block and a half before the finish) and the Marathon Sports store (approximately fifty feet before the finish line). In 2013, on the sidewalk in front of both establishments, lives were tragically lost and changed forever when bombs were detonated during the race. After 26.2 miles and endless challenges, it is the resolve, remembrance, and return that honor the race, the city, the people, and the country. It is worth remembering.

Once runners complete the Boston Marathon and pass under the media bridge, within the next two and a half blocks—from Dartmouth Street to Berkeley Street—is where official finishers can receive whatever they might need. Coordinating this are volunteers on the street and also a few sitting atop lifeguard towers situated in the middle of the road.

First up on Dartmouth is the main medical tent to the right of the runners, followed by the VIP tent just beyond it on Copley Square. Between Dartmouth and Clarendon Streets can be found water and sports drinks, and within the next block between Clarendon and Berkeley Streets are Heatsheet blankets, bags of food, and finishers' medals. On Berkeley, runners can pick up bags that were dropped off in Hopkinton.

Changing tents are located on Berkeley, the street that also serves as the exit to the family meeting areas that are marked with posted signs of the alphabet along Stuart Street and parts of Clarendon Street and St. James Avenue.

To top off the day—the accomplishment, the experience—a visit to the Boston Marathon Centennial Monument on Copley Square can put into focus the connection a finisher has with the legendary race's history. Located at the northwest corner of Boylston and Dartmouth, the mostly

An aerial view of the Boston Marathon finish line on Boylston Street, with the Boston Public Library in the foreground. *Photo by Paul C. Clerici.*

The two finish lines of the Boston Marathon—the laminated version seen on race day that is being placed over the painted one that is seen all the other days. *Photo by Paul C. Clerici.*

flat seven-ton granite monument is partially hidden between the medical and VIP tents.

In the middle of four points of pink marble posts is a wide multicolored granite medallion on the ground that features the names of every winner of the men's, women's, men's wheelchair, women's wheelchair, men's masters, and women's masters races since the beginning in 1897. The beauty of its design is that the names will remain etched in stone for years to come.

CHAPTER 10

MEMORIAL

As with most large-scale athletic events like marathons, whose fields can reach tens of thousands, injuries are inevitable and can include anything from dehydration and hypothermia to broken bones and cardiac episodes. Unfortunately, athlete deaths also can occur, as evidenced by the 1996 Boston Marathon, in which sixty-one-year-old Humphry Siesage died of a heart attack, and the 2002 Boston Marathon, when twenty-eight-year-old Cynthia Lucero died from hyponatremic encephalopathy.

But at the 117th Boston Marathon on April 15, 2013, three spectators—Krystle Campbell, twenty-nine; Lu Lingzi, twenty-three; and Martin Richard, eight—were fatally wounded within blocks of the finish line in a bombing attack that also injured 265 people. At approximately 2:50 p.m.—4:09:43 on the finish-line timing clock—two homemade pressure-cooker bombs were detonated on crowded Boylston Street within seconds of each other.

The first bomb exploded less than one hundred feet before the finish line, on the sidewalk area in front of the Marathon Sports store. The wide concourse walkway instantly took on the look of a war zone, with plumes of smoke, strewn shattered glass and debris, and fatally wounded and traumatically injured marathon spectators filling the area.

The second bomb, just seconds later, exploded less than four hundred feet after the twenty-six-mile mark, in front of the Forum bar and restaurant. Located about a block and a half west of the finish line, with a frontage sidewalk area smaller than that at Marathon Sports, similar tragic results were inflicted on the assembled spectators, bystanders, and alfresco diners.

After brief moments of disbelief, doubt, and comprehension passed, marathoners, spectators, and emergency personnel alike began to process and understand the magnitude of the occurrence as the smell of sulfur, cries of pain, and yells for help replaced the cheers and festive mood.

According to Nick Martin, director of communications for the Boston Public Health Commission, the three fatal victims succumbed to their injuries at the explosion sites and were not transported to a hospital. The 265 people who suffered nonfatal (but critical, serious, fair, etc.) injuries were either administered to in the medical tents at the corner of Boylston and Dartmouth Streets and/or were transported and treated at twenty-seven local and area hospitals. The most critical victims were sent to adult Level 1 trauma centers Boston Medical Center, Beth Israel Deaconess Medical Center, Brigham and Women's Hospital, Massachusetts General Hospital, and Tufts Medical Center, the latter of which also features a children's pediatric trauma center.

Thanks to quick-responding volunteers, medical and emergency personnel, and spectators, the injured swiftly received medical attention at the bombsites and also were transferred with extreme haste via continuous lines of moving wheelchairs streaming back and forth from the nearby medical tents to awaiting EMTs, paramedics, physicians, doctors, nurses, and ambulances. Reportedly, every person who received medical care survived his or her injuries.

Regarding the thousands of marathoners still on the course who were initially unaware of any emergency, quick logistical assessments resulted in the redirecting of runners.

First, Boylston Street was shut down at Hereford. Then, those on Hereford and Commonwealth were either briefly redirected down Commonwealth to the Boston Public Garden (seven blocks eastward) or halted completely. Soon, as the magnitude registered and officials conferred, the Boston Marathon was stopped.

The thousands of runners on Commonwealth Avenue—near and under the Massachusetts Avenue bridge overpass and also at Kenmore Square—were at a standstill. Word quickly spread throughout the course. Those still running were swiftly evacuated off the roads, some into impromptu places of shelter. In total, there were 5,633 official participants who were stopped prior to crossing the finish line.

Immediately—after people were treated and everyone evacuated from the area—a large fifteen-block crime-scene perimeter surrounding Boylston was closed off for the investigation. From west to east, it included Newbury Street (from Hereford to Berkeley) to the north of Boylston; Huntington

Part of the memorial at Copley Square was a fence of running shoes left in support of the victims of the 2013 bombings. *Photo by Paul C. Clerici.*

Avenue (from Belvidere Street to Berkeley via St. James Avenue) to the south of Boylston; Newbury to Huntington (by way of Hereford, Boylston, Dalton Street, Belvidere) to the west of Boylston; and Berkeley (from Newbury to St. James) to the east of Boylston.

Equally as immediate was the inception of the charitable The One Fund Boston foundation—jointly created by Massachusetts governor Deval Patrick and Boston mayor Thomas Menino; legislation for and acceptance of an official "Boston Strong" license plate, with a portion of the fees donated to the fund; and the physical show of support for the 3 victims who died and the 265 people who were injured.

At nearly every closed-off street that intersected Boylston could be found growing memorials of flowers, handmade signs, balloons, running shoes, and everything else imaginable draped on and around the gray metal police barricades. No greater were these personal expressions gathered than at the two opposite ends of Boylston—three and a half blocks to the west, at the corner of Hereford and Dalton, and two and a half blocks to the east, at the corner of Berkeley.

While it was an eerie sight to look down each end of Boylston and see everything in the exact same spot as it was from the explosions—toppled

Above: Looking east down a closed-off Boylston Street and the finish line, investigators searched for evidence after the bombings in 2013. *Photo by Paul C. Clerici.*

Left: At the memorial site on the corner of Boylston and Berkeley Streets, two children add their messages to the items left in support of the 2013 bombing victims. *Photo by Paul C. Clerici.*

barricades; barrels, trash, and signs spread all over the street; broken and crooked signposts and Marathon banners; and crime-scene tape—it was also reassuring (and a bit unnerving) to see so many law enforcement officers and investigators combing the area, collecting evidence and meticulously analyzing each block.

At Hereford and Dalton, bouquets of flowers lined the barricades, a stark juxtaposition to the nearby military vehicle standing sentry at the northwest exterior corner of the Hynes Convention Center. Posters, banners, and signs of support from local towns such as Wellesley, faraway states like Tennessee and California, and various countries were affixed to the fencing alongside American flags and dozens of handmade paper tulips with well wishes and prayers written on each. People came to pray, pay their respects, and share the pain but also to lend a hand, offer support, and provide strength. The power of the people was tangible throughout the city.

The city's area code of 617 and the phrase "Boston Strong" quickly began to appear everywhere—signs, shirts, hats, bracelets, cookies, stickers, pins, car magnets, and in spirit. Boston's professional sports teams—the Red Sox, Celtics, Bruins, New England Patriots, and New England Revolution—and many college teams incorporated the phrase and accompanying logo on jerseys (some as Boston 617 Strong), helmets, hats (some as B Strong), T-shirts, etc.

At Berkeley, from where the majority of the daily and nightly TV news reports originated, the site soon became a touchstone of emotion. It was where there were placed three small handmade white wooden crosses that featured the name of each person who died, and to them were attached a red heart and their pictures. It was where notes and letters with condolences and get-well wishes were placed. It was where teddy bears, running shoes, and candles were left. It was also where, quite often, children too young to understand the full impact sat down on the street and wrote special words with their crayons on pieces of paper they brought with them and added to the others.

It was beautiful, touching, and strengthening all at the same time.

For ten days, even as the perimeter was methodically reduced and some streets began to open up to traffic, the memorials continued to grow. When Boylston was finally open—first to business owners and later to the public—the largest of the memorials was moved to the adjacent sidewalk at Berkeley for a short period of time before a larger location at Copley Square was cleared and created with an enclosure of barricades where people could visit and continue to leave items.

The largest makeshift memorial, at the corner of Boylston and Berkeley Streets, became an emotional and cathartic beacon after the bombings in 2013. *Photo by Paul C. Clerici.*

There was a section of hundreds of running shoes—very personal expressions from runner to runner—that were laced up and over the top of the barricades, messages written on the sides. Singlets from track clubs, road races, and marathons were also hung up with pride. American flags, foreign flags, sports jerseys, hats and caps, mounds of stuffed animals, and personalized posters, cards, pennants, and letters were tied, taped, tucked, and placed everywhere. The support was overwhelming, appreciated, and welcomed.

While this combined memorial was closer to the bombing sites than the others, it also provided the healing and overtaking of what was once taken over. People patronized the stores and businesses that were closed since the Marathon. Smaller memorials bloomed in front of the Forum (flowers, signs, rosary beads) and Marathon Sports (flowers, messages, small crosses). While some damage marks on the sidewalks and storefronts remained as a sad reminder, the sight of a bustling and busy city was refreshing and warming. It was needed.

On several occasions, city officials removed the more delicate pieces and even covered up some of them during inclement weather. The memorial remained at Copley Square for two months—from April 24 to June 25—and was delicately taken to the City of Boston Archives, where previously removed items had been stored for categorizing, archiving, and viewing. Prior to its removal, Governor Patrick accompanied British prime minister David Cameron to the site, where the two paid their respects. Also, a few days after the bombings was held an interfaith service that was attended by, among others, President Barack Obama and First Lady Michelle Obama, both of whom later visited victims at separate hospitals.

Fundraising events, games, and performances were held to recognize first responders and victims while also serving as benefits. For a sense of closure, several "races" were held over the last portion of the course. And just over six weeks after the attack, a nearly six-hour star-studded Boston Strong Concert was held at the TD Garden.

The unending and massive amount of support was an indication to the BAA of the enormous interest and determination directed toward the 2014 Boston Marathon. It signaled the BAA, already in preparation, to rethink its field size, entrant requirements, and overall handling of the 118th running. Not only would it have to accommodate as many people as possible while also showing sensitivity to the resources of the eight cities and towns along the course, but it would also have to increase the safety and security of all those involved and do so with the utmost respect, integrity, and honor.

With that, the field was expanded to some 36,000 marathoners (up from about 27,000 in 2013). The 5,633 official entrants from 2013 who had reached at least the halfway point in Wellesley and were stopped prior to crossing the finish line received special invitations to run, and to those affected by the bombings, an exceptional allowance provided them the opportunity to express their special connection in writing for a possible entry.

In honor of the fatal victims, Massachusetts Bay Community College created the Krystle Campbell Scholarship Fund (she was a 2005 graduate), Boston University created the Lu Lingzi Scholarship Fund (she was a graduate student at BU), and the family of Martin Richard created the Martin W. Richard Charitable Foundation. Also, Massachusetts Institute of Technology (MIT) police officer Sean Collier was killed during the subsequent investigation and manhunt three days after the bombings. In his honor, MIT has created the Sean A. Collier Memorial Fund.

Regarding a permanent memorial, a Remembrance Committee was formed by the City of Boston to plan and ensure a proper tribute.

BIBLIOGRAPHY

Associated Press. "Fluid Cited in Marathoner's Death." August 13, 2002.

Boston Athletic Association (BAA). *Boston Marathon Media Guide(s)*. Boston: Boston Athletic Association with John Hancock, 2010–13.

Derderian, Tom. *The Boston Marathon: A Century of Blood, Sweat, and Cheers*. Chicago: Triumph Books, 2003.

———. *Boston Marathon: The First Century of the World's Premier Running Event*. Centennial Race Edition. Champaign, IL: Human Kinetics, 1996.

Longman, Jere. "MARATHON; Pippig Comeback Keeps Kenyans from a Sweep." *New York Times*, April 16, 1996.

Nason, Jerry. *The Story of the Boston Marathon from 1897*. Boston: *Boston Globe*, 1965.

Olsin, Reid. "University to Purchase Property." *Boston College Chronicle*, April 29, 2004.

Pave, Marvin. "Legacy on the Line." *Boston Globe*, April 17, 2008.

Squires, Bill, and Raymond Krise. *Fast Tracks: The History of Distance Running.* Brattleboro, VT: Stephen Greene Press, 1982.

Sullivan, Mark. "New Chapter in a Shared History." *Boston College Chronicle,* April 29, 2004.

Tye, Larry. "Dishonesty Has Long, Inglorious History." *Boston Globe,* April 17, 1998.

WEBSITES

Unless otherwise noted below or within the text, websites were used for general histories.

Archdiocese of Boston
The Ashland Estate of Henry Clay
Ashland Historical Society
Bank of America Chicago Marathon
Boston Art Commission
Boston Athletic Association (BAA)
Boston College
Boston Hotel Buckminster
Boston Red Sox ("Red Sox Notes," April 15, 2013)
Boston University ("Lu Lingzi Scholarship Fund," 2013)
Boulder Marathon
Brighton Allston Historical Society
Brookline Historical Society
Church of Saint Ignatius of Loyola
CITGO Petroleum Corporation
City of Boston
City of Newton
Framingham Historical Society
General Court of the Commonwealth of Massachusetts, 188th session (Bill H.3503, 2013)
Harvard University (*Arnoldia,* December 12, 1952)
Haynes Management Inc.

Hopkinton Historical Society
ING New York City Marathon (New York Road Runners Club press release, November 2, 2012)
Marathon Park (Ashland)
Marathon Run Museum (Greece)
Martin W. Richard Charitable Foundation
Massachusetts Bay Community College (Krystle Campbell Scholarship Fund, 2013)
Massachusetts Institute of Technology (MIT) (Sean A. Collier Memorial Fund, 2013)
Massachusetts Secretary of the Commonwealth Division of Public Records ("Report on the Custody and Condition of the Public Records of Parishes, Towns, and Countries," 1889)
Massachusetts Trial Court Law Libraries (*Boston Athletic Association vs. International Marathons Inc. & Others*, 392 Mass. 356, March 8, 1984–July 3, 1984)
MetroPCS Dallas Marathon
Natick Historical Society
National Aeronautics and Space Administration (NASA) (Press release, April 16, 2007)
Newton Historical Society
The Paul Revere House/Paul Revere Memorial Association
Prudential Center
St. Jude Memphis Marathon (Blog, December 10, 2013)
Town of Ashland
Town of Brookline
Town of Framingham
Town of Hopkinton
Town of Marathon (Greece)
Town of Natick
Town of Wellesley
26.2 Foundation
USA Track & Field (USATF) (Press release, April 20, 2008)
Visit Marathon (Greece)
Wellesley College
Wellesley Historical Society

INDEX

ABOUT THE AUTHOR

Paul C. Clerici, author of the *History of the Greater Boston Track Club* (The History Press), is a freelance journalist, writer, photographer, and former newspaper editor and sports editor who has been recognized in the *Who's Who in the East* publication. He has written for the *Foxboro Reporter* and *Walpole Times* newspapers, as well as for the *Boston College Chronicle, Level Renner, New England Patriots Weekly, New England Runner, North End Magazine, Orlando Attractions Magazine, Running Times,* and *State Street Journal* magazines and has produced shows at Walpole Community Television. A New England Press Association and Massachusetts Press Association award winner, he is also a regular contributor to *Marathon & Beyond* magazine. The race director of the Camy 5K Run & David 5K Walk, he has competed in nearly every distance from the mile to the marathon—including two triathlons, forty-three marathons, and twenty-three consecutive Boston Marathons—and has won several age-group and Clydesdale awards. A graduate of Curry College, the Walpole High School Hall of Fame member resides in his Massachusetts hometown.

Photo by Carol Hunt-Clerici.

Visit us at
www.historypress.net
....
This title is also available as an e-book

CPSIA information can be obtained
at www.ICGtesting.com
Printed in the USA
LVOW04*1523270717
542864LV00019B/269/P